Coastal Forces Vessels
of the Royal Navy from 1865

Coastal Forces Vessels
of the Royal Navy from 1865

MP Cocker

TEMPUS

M.P. Cocker contributes to the funds of the Imperial War Museum and the National Maritime Museum by being a Friend. Both of these fine nautical establishments are open to the public.

First published 2006

Tempus Publishing Limited
The Mill, Brimscombe Port,
Stroud, Gloucestershire, GL5 2QG
www.tempus-publishing.com

British Library Cataloguing in Publication Data.
A catalogue record for this book is available from the British Library.

ISBN 0 7524 3862 X

Typesetting and origination by Tempus Publishing Limited
Printed in Great Britain

Contents

Books by the same author

Title	Publisher
Destroyers of the Royal Navy 1893–1981	Ian Allan Ltd
Observer's Directory of Royal Naval Submarines	
Foreword by Vice Admiral Sir Lancelot Bell Davies	Fredk Warne Ltd
Frigates, Sloops and Patrol Vessels of the Royal Navy	
Foreword by HRH Prince Philip KG KT	Westmoreland Gazette
Mine Warfare Vessels of the Royal Navy	Airlife Ltd
(All out of print at September 2002)	
West Coast Support Group TG 96.8 Korea 1950–1953	
Foreword by Vice Admiral Sir Edward Anson	Whittles Ltd

In Preparation
Aircraft Carrying Ships of the Royal Navy 1908 to date

Some ships and craft of HM Fleet are included herein from my out of print earlier books, entitled *Mine Warfare Vessels*, and *Frigates, Sloops and Patrol Vessels*, being closer to the definition of Coastal Forces Vessels than as previously entered.

The earlier text has, in some classes, been updated and a number of photographs have been changed.

Foreword

It has been well said that small is beautiful. Although half a century has now passed since I did my national service with the Royal Navy, I am in no doubt that the part I enjoyed most was my time in HMS *Hornet* at Gosport. After a stint as First Lieutenant of a captured German E boat – 5212 – I was lucky enough to finish with my own command, HMS *Gay Charger*. I am sure that all who, like me, look back warmly on their service in Coastal Forces will welcome this book.

The Rt Hon. Lord Lawson
2006

Acknowledgements

I am deeply indebted to the following individuals and/or institutions, for help and advice during the compilation of this book. Additionally, I am grateful for permission to use their drawings and photographs and for the provision of the same. Listed in random order: Fairey Allday Marine Ltd, Cammell Laird Shipbuilders, Seaforth Maritime Ltd, J. Rosewarn, Royal Institution of Naval Architects, Lt Com. M.R. Wilson RN (Retd), Naval Historical Branch MOD(N), P. Kemp (Department of Photographs) Imperial War Museum, W.G. Clouter, Vickers Shipbuilding & Engineering Co. Ltd, W.C. McMillan, Yarrow (Shipbuilders) Ltd, P.J. Usher, Vosper Thornycroft (UK) Ltd, Wright & Logan, I. Hendry, Hall Russell & Co., Cmdr F.E.R. Phillips RN (Retd), N&M Chidgey, S. Freeman of Halmatic Ltd, G. Gifford of Griffon Hovercraft Ltd.

If, by any chance, I have omitted any individual or organisation, I trust that an apology will be accepted and understood.

List of Outline Drawings

Introduction

Within this illustrated reference book, mention is made with text, photographs and line drawings, of some of the lesser types of ships of the Royal Navy, varying from the large calibre gun monitors of both world wars to the commissioned armed launches which flew the White Ensign on Lake Tanganyika to the gas turbine-powered hovercraft of recent years. All have one similarity in that none were designed for action across the deep oceans of the world, even though many Coastal Forces vessels did transit the high seas to reach their theatre of operations.

As in my previous works, also listed are the many ships which were used by the Royal Navy although not originally designed or built for the same. Likewise, ships of the Empire Navies, now known as the Commonwealth, are excluded, excepting where continuity is required. Perhaps this book will be of interest as a reminder of the many losses incurred by these craft, which are listed with full loss details given, where known, of each casualty.

As to the damage inflicted against the enemy, many of these actions resulted in damage to vessels of both sides but, happily, many of our craft lived to fight another day. However, records are sparse on the damage inflicted to the enemy's mercantile marine, which largely formed the targets of the Dover Patrol and the Harwich Force of the First World War and Coastal Forces of the Second World War.

Today there are few vessels of the Coastal Forces breed in commission. They are a type which has largely passed from the scene, the fleet now lacking Monitors, Torpedo Boats, Motor Launches, Motor Gun and Torpedo Boats – such Landing Craft that are with the fleet are completely unarmed. However I hope this record of what is largely the past, is of interest and that it may commemorate Coastal Forces for the future.

M.P. Cocker
Lancashire
2006

Glossary

'A' Bracket	A metal bracket proud of the underwater hull holding the outer propeller shaft rigid	HMNZS	His Majesty's New Zealand Ship
AA	Anti-Aircraft	HMSAS	His Majesty's South African Ship
A/S	Anti-Submarine	HMS	His/Her Majesty's Ship
bhp	Brake Horse Power	hp	Horse Power
BL	Breech Loading	ihp	Indicated Horse Power
Calibre	The diameter of a missile, e.g. 4.7", 21"	INS	Indian Naval Ship
		LA	Low angle
Class	A number of ships all to the same design	LOA	Length overall
		LV	Light vessel
CP	Centre pivot (a gun mounting)	MA/SB	Motor Anti/Submarine Boat
DCT	Director Control Tower OR Depth Charge Thrower	mg	machine gun
		MGB	Motor Gun Boat
		M/L	Minelayer
		ML	Motor Launch
Displacement tons	The amount of water displaced in tons by a ship.	mm	millimetre
		MLR	muzzle loading rifle (gun)
DP	Dual purpose	MOD(N)	Ministry of Defence (Navy)
E-boat	A light tonnage (fast patrol boat) enemy surface craft	M/S	Minesweeper/minesweeping
		MTB	Motor Torpedo Boat
fps	Feet per second (speed of a projectile)	mtg	mounting
		mv	muzzle velocity
Full load tons	The displacement tonnage of a warship plus the weight of ammunition, fuel and stores	MV	Motor Vessel
		nm	nautical mile
		pdr	pounder
		P No.	pennant (Pendant) number
HA	High angle	pp	length between perpendiculars
HDML	Harbour Defence Motor Launch	QF	quick firing
HIMS	His Imperial Majesty's Ship (Japan)	RAN	Royal Australian Navy
		RCN	Royal Canadian Navy
HMAS	His Majesty's Australian Ship	RDF	Radio Direction Finding
HMCS	His Majesty's Canadian Ship	RHN	Royal Hellenic Navy

RIM	Royal Indian Marine	*TB*	Torpedo Boat	
R Neth N	Royal Netherlands Navy	*TBD*	Torpedo Boat Destroyer	
RNN	Royal Norwegian Navy	*TC*	Torpedo Catcher	
RNZN	Royal New Zealand Navy	*TBC*	Torpedo Boat Catcher	
R/T	Radio Telephony	*TD*	Torpedo Destroyer	
SANF	South African Naval Force	*Tubes*	Torpedo tubes	
SB	Smooth Bore	*U-boat*	Any enemy submarine	
SGB	Steam Gun Boat	*wl*	water line (length only)	
shp	shaft horse power	*W/T*	Wireless Telegraphy	
S/M	Submarine	*Yard*	(for shipbuilding yard)	
SS	Steam Ship			

Notes

Excepting where otherwise stated, all line drawings are of the coastal vessel design as conceived, and photographs of the ships as commissioned.

All lengths are overall.

All dimensions are in imperial measure, i.e. feet and inches, with tons of 2,240lb.

Type is the definition of the intended purpose of the vessel.

Machinery is the method of mechanical propulsion to and of the engines for propelling the vessel.

Complement is the total number of naval personnel in the ship's company.

Shaft means propeller shaft.

U-boat means any enemy submarine.

Coastal Forces vessels are or were commissioned into the Royal Navy; Commonwealth Navies vessels are not listed, excepting where a specific mention is made in the text.

The line drawings on several of the Class pages are reproduced by kind permission of the Royal Institution of Naval Architects, and are taken from the paper 'Warships 1860–1960' by the late President of the Institution, Sir Alfred Sims, and are all to the same scale. For details of other drawings see page 8.

Coastal Forces Vessels

The Royal Navy grew in strength and reputation by knowledge of the oceans of the world but any ship, irrespective of size, type and armament, must eventually return to base. With the British Empire so large in the Victorian era, the bases of our many fleets, both at home and overseas, had to be protected against any chance encounter with a possible enemy and the ships which were not for blue water sailing, but for guarding the coasts and harbours, fit very well under the title of Coastal Forces.

With the transition from sail to steam, steel-clad wooden vessels and iron-hulled ships of low power but adequate armament were deployed to be a coastguard fleet throughout the empire.

With the invention and deployment of the torpedo at least forty years prior to the advent of the submarine and the sea mine, the returning battleships and cruisers could be challenged by home-based flotillas of speedy torpedo boats which quickly outpaced any other ships and could quickly attack and disengage to return to their coastal base. The Torpedo Boats, whether of triple expansion or turbine engine propulsion, were of restricted range for operations and were less expensive than a cruiser for defence purposes. To back up the Torpedo Boats there were the slower Gun Boats and Monitors with heavier armament and stronger hulls which were, in turn, protected by the Torpedo Boats and the later coastal destroyers.

In the early part of the last century the internal combustion engine became so reliable that shortly after the commencement of the First World War, even faster craft were developed. Coastal Motor Boats were armed largely for torpedo warfare and the slower and steadier Motor Launches for many multifarious tasks. Throughout the world the Royal Navy had duties in large estuaries and rivers where shallow draft, medium speed and medium armament were required for the better keeping of the peace, backed up by the larger Monitors with heavier armament. A type of vessel had evolved to catch the Torpedo Boats known as the Torpedo Catcher. For all its own armament of medium guns and torpedoes, it lacked the speed, yet was able to deploy as an offshore gun vessel in its own right.

With the experience of the successful CMBs, Motor Launches and River Gun Boats, and the effectiveness of long range heavy monitor fire well proven, the First World War came to a close. However the CMBs and medium Monitors were still active against the Bolsheviks in North Russia up to 1920, and the existing and later River Gun Boats cruised the Tigris, Euphrates, Yangtse, Irrawaddy and other rivers on which ships flying the Red Ensign habitually traded.

At the home ports the older Monitors and surplus small craft were disposed of while the original but updated CMB design boats were still building in the UK for other nations up to the commencement of the Second World War. This found the Royal Navy with a few modern Motor Torpedo and Motor Gun Boats and a new type known as Motor Anti-Submarine Boats, all of high speed and better gun armament than in the First World War. But again the enemy had learned a lesson and produced the diesel-engined S-boat which had less of a tendency to catch fire, and was armoured in part, with high speed and dimensions superior to any RN Coastal Forces craft until the Fairmile 'D' Type arrived, supplemented a little by the lightly armoured steel Steam Gun Boats with light to semi-medium guns and torpedoes.

The Second World War was very widespread and, although the conquest, or re-conquest, of occupied territory is largely a task for the Army, it is the Navy that delivers the troops and their associated vehicles and armour to the coast which has to be taken. New craft were designed for the landing of troops over open beaches and the new Landing Craft were defended by Landing Craft 'Monitors' with guns equal to any destroyer and able to project from some craft a rocket bombardment which, subject to accuracy, was of great effectiveness and a morale booster. The new Monitors and newer MGB and MTBs and River Gun Boats of the Second World War were all of superb design and many new types and classes saw service. But, with the Allied victory, the River Gun Boats and Monitors were laid up and later sold, the war-built MGB and MTBs with their supporting sisters, the 'B' Motor Launches and Harbour Defence Motor Launches, were largely decommissioned and paid off and others were disposed of by sale or tender.

New Coastal Forces classes were designed and built, the majority of these new buildings being named, although still wearing a pendant number as tradition dictated. Propulsion throughout the Second World War had largely been by petrol engines, but the new classes were mainly diesel engined and built as Interchangeable MGB/MTBs, similar to the 'D' Type Fairmile design of the war. Construction now changed from wooden craft to composite and all-aluminium, and the gas turbine engine installed in some classes permitted speeds hardly reached by the hydrofoil HMS *Speedy* of the late 1970s.

By 1950, the armament of Coastal Forces vessels abroad was entering the missile stage, which foretold the sinking of the ex-British, Israeli Destroyer *Elath* by a missile from a Russian designed and built OSA patrol vessel of the Egyptian Navy. The missile had been aimed, from over the horizon and miles away, by the new electronic radar weapon systems developed by the Iron Curtain countries. Suddenly, and for no apparent reason, apart from the view of HMG that other matters were worthier of funding, the ships of the Royal Naval Coastal Forces were decommissioned and sent for disposal. Three new hulls were budgeted for training, with an optimum of weapon fits, but only small arms were carried. In 1984 HMS *Cutlass, Sabre* and *Sceptre* were for sale. Likewise the Hovercraft, which still displayed an element of speed, were for disposal – only those with a Mine Counter Measures capability being retained for a while. The 'Ford' Seaward Anti-Submarine Craft had a good A/S capability but lacked the range and seaworthiness of a U-boat-hunting Frigate, despite being armed with ahead-throwing weapons and a modern Asdic outfit. The Jetfoil *Speedy* was tried and found wanting, ending its service on fishery protection duties with the 'Peacock' Class of five, commissioned to guard Hong Kong. Not so far into their commissions, they were sold, two to Eire and three to the Philippines Navy with their modern automatic 76mm main armament. The RAF Marine Branch lost its craft to the Royal Navy in 1986 and the Royal Marines acquired new small Hovercraft and high speed narrow hulls for covert operations from 1994. Little remains of the Coastal Force as it was in the First and Second World Wars but on one of the memorials to those who crewed these craft, the following verse can be found:

Here dead we lie because we did not choose
To live and shame the land from which we sprung
Life to be sure is nothing much to lose
But young men think it is and we were young.

Chapter 1

Coastal Defence Ships and Monitors

HMS *Royal Sovereign*, Coast Defence Ship

HMS	Commenced	Completed	Builder
Royal Sovereign	1849	1864	HM Dockyard, Portsmouth

Specification

Displacement tons	5,080
Dimensions	240½pp x 62 x 23¼
Armament	Five 10.5in SB guns on three single and one twin mounting
Machinery	One horizontal compound engine to one shaft giving 2,460ihp
Speed	11 knots
Armour	Minimum 1in deck to 10in on the turrets
Complement	300

Note: HMS *Royal Sovereign* was the first operational turret ship and was laid down as a three-deck ship of 121 guns but was substantially altered prior to completion in 1862.

Weapon note: The 10.5in gun fired a round shot projectile of 150lb. The single turrets weighed 151 tons and the twin turret 164 tons. An armoured conning tower was fitted.

Fate: *Royal Sovereign* was sold for breaking up in 1885.

Royal Sovereign. (National Maritime Museum)

Prince Albert. (National Maritime Museum)

HMS *Prince Albert*, Coast Defence Ship

HMS	Commenced	Completed	Builder
Prince Albert	1862	1866	Samuda Poplar

Specification

Displacement tons	3,687
Dimensions	240pp x 48 x 19¾
Armament	Four 9in MLR guns all in single centreline turrets
Machinery	One direct action engine to one shaft giving 2,128ihp
Speed	11¼ knots
Armour	Minimum 1⅛in upper deck to 10½in on the turrets
Complement	201

Note: HMS *Prince Albert* was the first iron turret ship for the Royal Navy with her protection similar to HMS *Royal Sovereign* (1864).

Weapon note: The guns were hand worked and each of the complete turrets (from the six originally intended) weighed 112 tons. The conning tower which was not armoured was positioned aft of the foremast before the funnel.

Fate: HMS *Prince Albert* remained in the fleet until 1899 by command of Her Majesty, but was sold for breaking up in the same year.

HMS *Abyssinia*, Coast Defence Monitor

HMS	Commenced	Completed	Builder
Abyssinia	1868	1870	Dudgeon Poplar

Specification

Displacement tons	2,901
Dimensions	225pp x 42 x 14½
Armament	Four 10in MLR guns in two twin turrets
Machinery	Two Dudgeon engines to two shafts all giving 1,200ihp
Speed	9½ knots
Armour	Minimum of 6in on the belt to 10in on the turrets
Complement	100

Note: HMS *Abyssinia* was an austerity version of the 'Cerberus' Class listed below. She served as a coast defence ship at Bombay where she remained for her entire series of commissions. A conning tower was fitted forward of the funnel.

Fate: Sold for breaking up in 1903 at Bombay.

'Cerberus' Class Coast Defence Monitors

HMS	Commenced	Completed	Builder
Cerberus (later *Platypus II*)	1867	1870	Palmers
Magdala	1868	1870	Thames Iron Works

Specification

Displacement tons	3,344
Dimensions	225pp x 45 x 15¼
Armament	Four 10in MLR in two twin turrets
Machinery	Two horizontal return engines all giving 1,369ihp with 1,436ihp for *Magdala*, to two shafts
Speed	*Cerberus* 9¾ knots and *Magdala* 10½ knots
Armour	Minimum 1in decks to 10in on the turrets
Complement	155

Cerberus. (National Maritime Museum)

Note: This was a design for a coastal defence ship to be based overseas and both ships had yards and sails for their outward delivery voyages.

Fate: *Cerberus* was sunk as a breakwater in 1926 at Melbourne and *Magdala* sold for breaking up in 1904.

Note: Gunvessels, Gun Boats and similar craft built for, and as a result of, the Crimean War and in response to the invasion scares of the period 1867–1875 are not included in this work.

HMS *Glatton*, **Coast Defence Monitor**

HMS	Commenced	Completed	Builder
Glatton	1868	1872	HM Dockyard, Chatham

Specification

Displacement tons	4,912
Dimensions	225pp x 45 x 14½
Armament	Two 12in MLR in one twin turret
Machinery	Two Lairds engines giving 2,870ihp to two shafts
Speed	12 knots
Armour	Minimum 1½in deck to 14in on the turret
Complement	185

Note: HMS *Glatton* was quite heavily armoured and built with a deep draught to enable her to undertake operations with the fleet at sea. She had almost an excess of 12¼ knots over her designed speed which was 9¾ knots.

Fate: Sold for breaking up in 1903.

Glatton. (National Maritime Museum)

'Cyclops' Class Coast Defence Monitors

HMS	Commenced	Completed	Builder
Cyclops	1870	1877	Thames Iron Works
Gorgon	1870	1874	Palmers
Hecate	1870	1877	Dudgeon
Hydra	1870	1876	Napier

Specification

Displacement tons	3,480			
Dimensions	225pp x 45 x 16¼			
Armament	Four 10in MLR in two twin turrets			
Machinery	*Gorgon & Hecate*		*Cyclops & Hydra*	
	Two cylinder horizontal direct acting engines to two shafts		Two cylinder compound engines to two shafts	
	Cyclops	*Gorgon*	*Hecate*	*Hydra*
Speed & ihp	11 knots	11 knots	10¾ knots	11¼ knots
	1,660	1,670	1,755	1,472
Armour	Minimum 1½in deck to 10in on the turrets			
Complement	150			

Note: May be described as repeat *Cerberus* ships but with modifications.
Fate: All sold for breaking up in 1903.

'Humber' Class River Monitors

HMS	Commenced	Completed	Builder
Humber (ex-*Javary*)	1912	1913	Vickers
Mersey (ex-*Madeira*)	1912	1914	Vickers
Severn (ex-*Solimoes*)	1912	1914	Vickers

Specification

Displacement tons	1,520 deep
Dimensions	266¾ x 49 x 5¾
Armament	Two 6in, two 4.72in Howitzers, four 3pdr, six 7mm Hotchkiss mg
Machinery	Twin screw triple expansion of 1,450ihp
Speed	12 knots (Designed) 9½ knots service
Range	2,800 at 8 knots
Fuel	187 tons coal and 90 tons of oil
Complement	140

Note: All of the above were under construction in England at the commencement of the
First World War for the Brazilian Navy but were taken over by the Admiralty.

Hydra. (National Maritime Museum)

Mersey. (Vickers SB&E)

HMS *Severn* and *Mersey* are well remembered for their deployment to the Rufiji River in German East Africa where the SMS *Konigsberg* had taken refuge from ships of the Royal Navy. With their shallow draft they were able to proceed some distance up the Rufiji estuary to a position where they could bombard the *Konigsberg*. It was out of sight of *Mersey* and *Severn* around many bends of the jungle-clad river banks, but with the aid of spotter aircraft of the Royal Naval Air Service (which also dropped a number of lightweight bombs) the target was set on fire and badly damaged by the W/T directed shoot of the Monitors and further damaged by further detonations by the German crew to disable their own ship. The remains of the *Konigsberg* are still visible in the Rufiji River today.

Fate: *Humber* was sold in 1920 and used as a crane barge by a Dutch salvage firm until about 1938, *Mersey* was scrapped at Morecambe in 1922 and *Severn* in 1923.

'M' Class, Coastal Monitors

HMS	Launched	Builder
M15	1915	Gray
M16	1915	Gray
M17	1915	Gray
M18	1915	Gray
M19	1915	Raylton, Dixon
M20	1915	Raylton, Dixon
M21	1915	Raylton, Dixon
M22 (later *Medea*)	1915	Raylton, Dixon
M23 (later *Claverhouse*)	1915	Raylton, Dixon
M24	1915	Raylton, Dixon
M25	1915	Raylton, Dixon
M26	1915	Raylton, Dixon
M27	1915	Raylton, Dixon
M28	1915	Raylton, Dixon
M29 (later *Medusa*) (later *Talbot*) (later *Medway II*) (later *Medusa*)	1915	Harland & Wolff
M30	1915	Harland & Wolff
M31 (later *Melpomene*) (later *Menelaus*)	1915	Harland & Wolff
M32	1915	Workman, Clark
M33 (later *Minerva*)	1915	Workman, Clark

Specification for Monitors M15, M16, M17, M18, M19, M20, M21, M22, M23, M24 M25, M26, M27 and M28

Displacement tons	650 deep for M15, M16, M17 and M18
	610 deep for M19 to M28 inclusive

M29. (Imperial War Museum)

M27. (World Ship Society)

M33. (Imperial War Museum)

Dimensions	173¼ x 31 x 7 for M15 to M18 inclusive
	173¼ x 31 x 6½ for M9 to M28 inclusive
Armament	One 9.2in, one 12pdr, one 6pdr Hotchkiss and two mgs for M15 to M28
Machinery	Twin screw triple expansion 800ihp for M15 to M17
	600ihp for M21
	650ihp for M22
	Twin screw semi-diesel engine 640bhp for M18, M19, M20, M23, M25 and M28
	Quadruple screw semi-diesels 480bhp for M26, 560bhp for M27
	Quadruple screw paraffin engines 640bhp for M24
Range	660nm at 9½ knots and 2,200mn at 9½ knots for oil-engined ships
Fuel	28 to 32 tons of fuel oil
Speed	12 knots (designed) and 11 knots service
Complement	69

Specification for Monitors M29, M30, M31, M32 and M33

Displacement tons	580 deep
Dimensions	177¼ x 31 x 6
Armament	Two 6in, one 6pdr Hotchkiss 2 mg
Machinery	Twin screw triple expansion 400ihp
Range	1,440nm at 8 knots
Fuel	45 tons of fuel oil
Speed	10 knots (designed) and 9 knots service
Complement	72

Experimental armament note: M27 had her 6in piece replaced by a triple 4in BIX (3x1) similar to the mountings on the Battle Cruiser HMS *Renown* and *Repulse* for service in the White Sea.

Note: Intended to be built to the one design but evolved as three versions with variants.

Armour: The 'M' Monitors were not armoured but for M19 to M28 the 9.2in gunshield had a 4in face and 1½in sides, with M29 to M33 having 3in on the face of the 6in gunshield.

Fates: M16, 18, 19, 20, 24, 26 and 32 were sold in 1920 for oil storage. HMS M22, M29, M31 and M33 were converted into minelayers in 1925. HMS M23 became an RNVR Drill Ship in 1922.

Losses: HMS M15 was torpedoed by UC38 off Gaza on 11 November 1917.
HMS M21 was mined off Osten on 20 October 1918.
HMS M25 was scuttled by own forces on the Dvina River, being blocked in by ice to avoid her being taken by Bolshevik forces on 16 September 1919, as was HMS M27.
HMS M28 was sunk after a surface action with the SMSs *Breslau* and *Goeben* off Imbros on 20 January 1918. HMS M30 was engaged and sunk by shore batteries in the Gulf of Smyrna on 13 May 1916.

'Abercrombie' Class Coast Defence Ships or Monitors

HMS	Commenced	Completed	Builder
Abercrombie	1914	1915	Harland & Wolff
(ex-*General Abercrombie*)			
(ex-*M1*)			
(ex-*Admiral Farragut*)			
(ex-*Farragut*)			
Havelock	1914	1915	Harland & Wolff
(ex-*M2*)			
(ex-*General Grant*)			
Raglan	1914	1915	Harland & Wolff, Govan
(ex-*Lord Raglan*)			
(ex-*M3*)			
(ex-*Robert E. Lee*)			
Roberts	1914	1915	Swan Hunter
(ex-*Earl Roberts*)			
(ex-*M4*)			
(ex-*Stonewall Jackson*)			

Raglan. (Imperial War Museum)

Specification

Displacement tons	6,150
Dimensions	334½ x 90¼ x 10
Armament	Two 14in, two 12pdr, one 3pdr, one 2pdr, four mgs
Aircraft	These monitors were designed to carry two float planes for spotting, probably the Sopwith 808, or similar type
Machinery	Reciprocating engines to two shafts giving 2,310ihp for *Raglan*, 1,800ihp for *Roberts* and *Abercrombie*. *Havelock* had quadruple expansion engines giving 2,000ihp
Speed	10 knots (designed) 6½ knots service
Range	1,340nm at 6 knots
Armour	4in deck and 10in on the main turret

Aircraft note: All designed to carry two seaplanes and fitted with aircraft handling derricks. These were positioned at the after end of the forecastle deck. During the Gallipoli bombardments, HMS *Raglan* and HMS *Roberts* operated a Short 166 aircraft and *Abercrombie* a Sopwith Schneider float plane. Later HMS *Raglan* carried a Short 184 which was transferred from the Kite Balloon ship *City of Oxford*.

Complement	198

Note: All very under powered and of low speed

Loss: HMS *Raglan* was sunk after a surface action with the SMSs *Breslau* and *Goeben* off Imbros, on 20 January 1918.

Fate: *Abercrombie* and *Havelock* sold 1927. *Roberts* sold 1936.

'Lord Clive' Class Coast Defence Ships or Monitors

HMS	Commenced	Completed	Builder
Earl of Peterborough (ex-M8)	1915	1915	Harland & Wolff
General Craufurd (ex-*Craufurd*) (ex-M7)	1915	1915	Harland & Wolff
General Wolfe (ex-*Sir James Wolfe*) (ex-*Wolfe*) (ex-M9)	1915	1915	Palmer
Lord Clive (ex-*Clive*) (ex-M6)	1915	1915	Harland & Wolff
Prince Eugene (ex-M11)	1915	1915	Harland & Wolff, Govan
Prince Rupert (ex-M10) (later *Pembroke*)	1915	1915	Hamilton

General Wolfe. (Imperial War Museum)

Prince Rupert. (Imperial War Museum)

Sir John Moore	1915	1915	Scotts
(ex-*M5*)			
Sir Thomas Picton	1915	1915	Harland & Wolff
(ex-*Picton*)			
(ex-*M12*)			

Specification

Displacement tons	5,900
Dimensions	335½ x 87¼ x 9½
Armament	Two 1in, two 12pdr, one 3pdr (except *Prince Eugene*)
	One 2pdr, (except *General Craufurd*) four mg, one 3in (*General Craufurd* and *Prince Eugene* only)
Machinery	Triple expansion engines; *General Wolfe* 2,500ihp, *Sir John Moore* 2,500ihp 3 cylinder, *Prince Rupert* 1,600ihp, others 2,310ihp all to two shafts
Speed	10 knots (designed) 7 knots service
Range	1,100nm at 6½knots
Fuel	356 tons coal
Armour	6in deck and 10in on the main turret

Aircraft note: During August 1916, HMS *General Craufurd*, while bombarding the Belgian coast (German occupied) operated a Short 184 for spotting the fall of shot

Complement	194

Note: These eight monitors were an improvement on the 'Abercrombie' Class but still with very low speed.

Fate: All sold in 1921 excepting *Prince Rupert* in 1923 and *Lord Clive* 1927.

'Marshall Ney' Class Coast Defence Ships or Monitors

HMS	Commenced	Completed	Builder
Marshall Ney	1915	1915	Palmer
(ex-*M13*)			
(later *Vivid*)			
(later *Drake*)			
(later *Alaunia* II)			
Marshall Soult	1915	1915	Palmer
(ex-*M14*)			

Specification

Displacement tons	6,670
Dimensions	355¾ x 90¼ x 10½
Armament	Two 15in, eight 4in, two 12pdr, two 3in AA, two 2pdr AA
Machinery	Diesel engines to two shafts (*Marshall Ney*) 1,500bhp (*Marshall Soult*) 1,520bhp
Speed	9 knots (designed) 6 knots service

Marshall Ney. (Imperial War Museum)

Marshall Soult. (Imperial War Museum)

Range	2,080nm at 5½ knots
Fuel	226 tons oil fuel
Armour	4in deck and 13in on the main turret
Complement	187

Note: Satisfactory ships, well protected but even slower than their predecessors. These Monitors were armed with the latest 15in guns and as a consequence were not scrapped until after the Second World War. Both were used for gunnery training. *Marshall Soult* was based at Portsmouth and *Marshall Ney* went to Devonport and Chatham.

Fate: *Marshall Ney* was broken up in 1957 and *Marshall Soult* in 1946.

Cancelled ships: Four of this class, designed for steam propulsion with a minimum of 10 knots speed and with four 15in guns, were ordered in May 1915. They were allocated the numbers M34 and M35 for Harland & Wolff's yard and M36 and M37 for Swan Hunter's Yard, but were all cancelled one month later.

'Erebus' Class, Coast Defence Ships or Monitors

HMS	Commenced	Completed	Builder
Erebus	1915	1916	Harland & Wolff, Govan
Terror	1915	1916	Harland & Wolff

Specification

Displacement tons	8,000
Dimensions	405 x 88 x 11
Armament	Two 15in, eight 4in, two 12pdr, two 3in, two 2pdr, four mg
Machinery	Triple expansion to two shafts giving 6,000ihp
Speed	12 knots. Both exceeded 13½ knots on trials
Range	2,480nm at 12 knots
Fuel	784 tons oil
Armour	5in deck to 12in on the main turret
Complement	204

Note: The most satisfactory design of large monitors from the First World War.

Fate: HMS *Erebus* was attached to Chatham Gunnery School and in 1919 became one of the supporting vessels for the Allies at Murmansk against the Bolshevik forces of Russia. Later she was in the Baltic but paid off at Chatham in 1921 as a Drill Ship. She was maintained in commission and saw service throughout the Second World War in the Mediterranean and other theatres of war.

Aircraft note: HMS *Terror* in 1937 on the Singapore station operated a Walrus amphibian. After the Second World War however, she was old and was broken up in 1947. HMS *Terror* was also too good a ship to dispose of and served as a Gunnery Trials ship in the 1920s and later as a Harbour Training Ship. With the commencement of World War II she had similar service to HMS *Erebus*. On 23 February 1941 she left Benghazi and was severely mined and at daybreak was attacked by German aircraft and sank off Derna.

Erebus. (Source not known)

Terror. (Imperial War Museum)

'Gorgon' Class, Coast Defence Ships

HMS	Commenced	Completed	Builder
Glatton (ex-*Bjoergvin*)	1913	1918	Armstrong
Gorgon (ex-*Nidaros*)	1913	1918	Armstrong

Specification

Displacement tons	6,150
Dimensions	310 x 73¾x 16½
Armament	Two 9.2in, six 6in, two 3in AA, four 2pdr AA
Machinery	Triple expansion to two shafts giving 4,000ihp
Speed	13 knots
Fuel	394 tons coal and 170 tons oil
Armour	From 2in on the deck to 8in on the turrets
Complement	303

Note: These were two Coast Defence Ships being built in England for the Norwegian Navy but taken over by the Admiralty and described as Monitors.

Fate: *Gorgon* sold 1928.

Loss: HMS *Glatton,* after an internal explosion, sank in Dover Harbour on 16 September 1918.

Glatton. (Imperial War Museum)

'Roberts' Class Monitors

HMS	Commenced	Completed	Builder
Abercrombie	1941	1943	Vickers Armstrong
Roberts	1940	1941	John Brown

Specification

Displacement tons	7,973 deep *Roberts* and 8,536 *Abercrombie*
Dimensions	373¼ x 89¾ x 13½
Armament	Two 15in, eight 4in DP AA on twin mtgs, sixteen 2pdr (two quad, one octuple mtgs)
	Eight 20mm AA *Abercrombie* and twenty 20mm AA *Roberts*
Machinery	Twin screw single reduction geared turbines for 4,800shp
Range	2,680nm at 12 knots
Fuel	491 tons of oil fuel
Speed	12¼ knots designed and service
Complement	442/460
Armour	Main deck 4in to 6in and 13in on the gunhouse

The last and most successful Monitors built for the Royal Navy.

Aircraft note: HMS *Abercrombie* and HMS *Roberts* had the capability to operate a Walrus amphibian.

Fate: *Abercrombie* was scrapped in 1954 and *Roberts* in 1965.

Abercrombie. (Imperial War Museum)

Roberts. (Imperial War Museum)

Normandy Bombardment Tower

Landing Craft (Gun) Tower, LC(G)T

HMS	Commenced	Completed	Builder
LC(G)T1	1943	1943	Derman Long & Sir Alex Gibb

Specification

Dimensions	Height from keel to top of structure 50ft. Length of twin hull 130 x 13 x 12½ keel to main deck
Armament	Two 6in Howitzers, four 20mm
Machinery	Two shaft diesel engines, one to each hull Leyland Bua pattern, say 300bhp overall
Complement	12

Note: Information obtained from the booklet by F.R. Turner of the title as above. When the early landing craft were constructed it was assumed that they would he under-gunned by the enemy beach defences. Therefore it was decided that the above craft, of which only one was built (although it had been intended that numbers would be commissioned), would act as a floating defence for the initial waves of LCAs and similar vessels which transported troops and armour to the Normandy beachheads. The LC(G)T was superseded by numerous support versions of the LCA LCT and LST versions already built and commissioned and in service.

Therefore the only version of the above was not deployed on operations. It was presumably being de-stored, de-ammunitioned, laid up then sold for breaking up (see Fate section).

Construction was of steel concrete and materials as used in the building trade but fitted out as to the standard of a Coastal Forces Vessel of the Royal Navy.

May be described as a semi-submersible austerity inshore Monitor.

Fate: Sold post-war and used as a lifting craft at Hong Kong.

Operation: On passage proceeded as a normal catamaran to within gun range of the enemy fortifications. The hulls were flooded to permit the craft to submerge so that only the gun-carrying superstructure was above sea level and only the 'turret' would be observed from the shore. After the engagement the hulls would be pumped dry and the craft would move out of range of the guns on shore or when the craft was low on ammunition, victualling and fuel.

Normandy Bombardment Tower, LC(G)T1. (F.R. Turner)

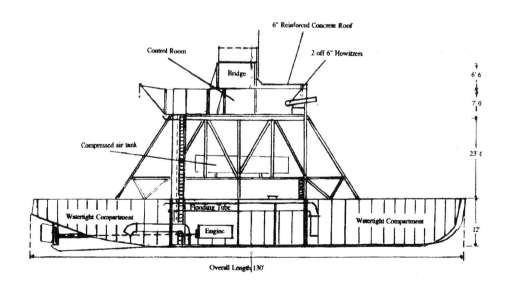

Landing Craft (Gun) Tower, longitudinal section.

Chapter 2

First and Second Class Torpedo Boats

HMS *Lightning*, Torpedo Boat

HMS	Completed	Builder
Lightning (later TB1)	1876	Thornycroft

Specification

Displacement tons	32
Dimensions	84½pp x 10¾ x 5¼
Torpedo carriers	Two carriers, one port and one starboard each for one 14in torpedo which could be lowered into the water, and the torpedo then released
Machinery	One compound engine to one shaft of 460ihp
Speed	19 knots
Complement	5 plus, according to occasion

Note: HMS *Lightning,* being first of class and first of type, was hardly a naval vessel by design, having originated from a traditional steam launch hull, but she was fast for her day and her armament was equal to the broadside of any ship of the fleet if her torpedoes struck the target ship – her lethality was obvious from the start. In 1879, the torpedo carriers were removed and she had one torpedo tube mounted on her

Lightning, later TB1. (Vosper Thornycroft)

forecastle deck with two reload torpedoes carried on trolleys in positions where the carriers had been. *Lightning* was used for countless evaluations, being used as a tender to the torpedo school HMS *Vernon*.

Fate: TB1 (name and number were used *inter alia*) was broken up at Portsmouth in 1896.

First Class Torpedo Boats built by J.I. Thornycroft

Torpedo Boats 2, 3, 4, 5, 6, 7, 8, 9, 10, 11 and 12

All built 1878–1879

Specification

Displacement tons	28
Dimensions	86½pp x 10¼ x 5¼, TB10 91pp x 10¼ x 5¼
Torpedo tube	One 14in with two reloads
Machinery	One compound engine to one shaft 460ihp
Speed	20 knots

Note: The follow on design from TB1, all fitted with the torpedo tube at the appropriate stage in construction.

Fates: All sold for breaking between 1894 and 1906.

Deployment: TB6 ended her days at the Cape, TB7 at Gibraltar, and TBs 8, 9, 10, and 11 at Hong Kong. HM TB10 was built with a ram bow and an alternate lined hull.

TB2. (Imperial War Museum)

Torpedo Boats 21 and 22

Built 1884–1885

Specification

Displacement tons	64
Dimensions	113½ x 12½ x 6
Armament	Two 3pdr
Torpedo tubes	Two 14in single tubes
Machinery	Triple expansion of 700ihp to one shaft
Speed	20 knots
Complement	14

Note: Two TBs showing how the type was increasing in potentiality and size.
Fate: Not known.

Torpedo Boat 25

Built 1885

Specification

Displacement tons	60
Dimensions	128½ x 12½ x 6
Armament	Two 1in twin Nordenfelt or two 3pdr
Torpedo tubes	Two twin 14in
Machinery	As TB21 but of 700ihp
Speed	21 knots
Complement	16

Note: Built with a ram bow which was later reconstructed.
Fate: Served throughout the First World War as a patrol vessel, broken up in 1919.

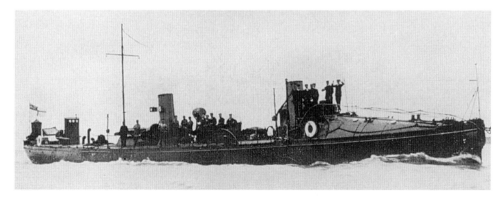

TB25. (Navpic)

Torpedo boats 26, 27, 28, 29, 41, 42, 43, 44, 45, 46, 47, 48, 49, 50, 51, 52, 53, 54, 55, 56, 57, 58, 59 and 60

All built 1885–1886

Specification

Displacement tons	All as TB25
Dimensions	All as TB25
Torpedo tubes	All as TB25
Machinery	All as TB25, but varied from 700–750ihp
Speed	As TB25, with speed varying from 19½ to 22 knots
Complement	16

Note: These TBs were similar in most respects to TB25 and achieved their best speed after the modification to the bow had been implemented by the dockyard to give a straight stem.

Fates: TBs 26 and 27 sold in 1919, likewise TB29, but at Capetown. TBs 41, 42 and 57 sold 1919 as were TBs 45, 54, 49, 52, 58 and 60. TBs 43 and 44 sold 1919 at Malta, TB48 sold 1915, TB60 sold 1919 at Capetown.

Loss: HM TB46 (later 0146), while in tow on 27 December 1915, went aground in the Eastern Mediterranean, but was later salvaged and broken up in 1920.

Naming note: In the period 1906 to 1909, with the continued building of torpedo boats, the figure 0 was added to the numbers of existing craft, thus HM TB26 became HM TB026.

TB26. (Vosper Thornycroft)

Torpedo Boats 91 and 92

Built 1892 to 1894

Specification

Displacement tons	141	
Dimensions	140½ x 15½ x 17½	TB91 142½ x 15½ x 17½
Armament	Three 3pdr	
Torpedo tubes	Three 18in single tubes	
Machinery	Triple expansion of 2,350ihp.	TB91 was of greater length than her sister, as an experiment to place the propeller further aft
Speed	24½ knots	
Complement	18	

Note: Both served throughout the First World War.
Fate: TB91 sold in 1919 and 92 sold 1920 at Gibraltar.

Torpedo Boat 93

Specification

Displacement tons	136
Dimensions	140½ x 15½ x 5
Armament	As TB91
Torpedo tubes	As TB91
Machinery	Twin triple expansion engines all giving 2,200ihp to two shafts
Speed	23½ knots
Complement	18

Note: HM TB93 was the first twin screw torpedo boat.
Fate: Sold in 1919.

Torpedo Boats 98, 99, 107 and 108

Built 1900–1901

Specification

Displacement tons	185
Dimensions	164 x 17 x 6
Armament	Three 3pdr
Torpedo tubes	Three 18in single tubes
Machinery	Triple expansion giving 3,000ihp
Speed	25 knots
Complement	32

TB91. (Vosper Thornycroft)

TB93. (Source not known)

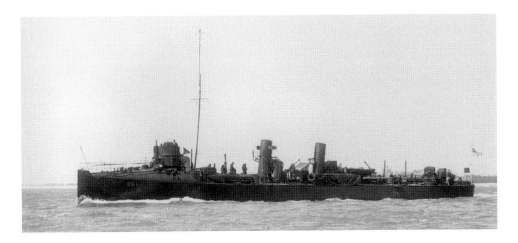

TB98. (Vosper Thornycroft)

Note: These four TBs proved to be very short ranged, with just six hours full speed steaming.

Fates: All broken up 1920.

Loss: HM TB99 foundered in heavy weather in 1907 but was raised and salvaged.

Torpedo Boats 109, 110, 111, 112, and 113

All built 1901–1903

Specification

Displacement tons	200
Dimensions	166 x 70¼ x 5½
Armament	Three 3pdr
Torpedo tubes	Three 18in single tubes
Machinery	Triple expansion 3,050ihp
Speed	25 knots
Complement	32

Note: All saw war service in the First World War.

Fates: TBs 109, 110,111 and 112 broken up in 1920. 113 was broken up in 1919.

TC109. (Vosper Thornycroft)

First Class Torpedo Boats built by J.S. White & Co.

Torpedo Boat 19

Built 1878

Specifications

Displacement tons	28
Dimensions	93 x 10¾ x 4
Torpedo tube	One 14in with two reloads
Machinery	One compound engine to one shaft 460ihp
Speed	21 knots
Complement	15

Note: TB19 was the first of these craft built by J.S. White.

Fate: Decommissioned in 1886 and broken up in 1899.

Torpedo Boats 34, 35, 36, 37 and 38

Built 1885–1887

Specifications

Displacement tons	60/66
Dimensions	125pp x 14½ x 4
Armament	As TB25
Torpedo tubes	As TB25
Machinery	Triple expansion 950ihp
Speed	20 knots
Complement	16

TB034. (Imperial War Museum)

Note: This version of TB had a 'cut up' stern which improved steering.

Fate: TBs 35, 36, 37 and 38 served at Hong Kong and were broken up there in 1919. TB34 was broken up in 1920.

Torpedo Boat 81, but purchased as SS *Swift*

Built 1884–1887

Specification

Displacement tons	137
Dimensions	153¾ x 17½ x 9½
Armament	Four 3pdr
Torpedo tubes	Three 14in
Machinery	Triple expansion 1,330ihp
Speed	23½ knots
Complement	25

Note: *Swift* was built as a private venture by Whites and in 1885 the Admiralty decided to purchase her, renaming her TB81. The completion was delayed but eventually she was commissioned as a Torpedo Boat, although consideration had been given to making her into a Torpedo Catcher.

Fate: Broken up in 1921.

Torpedo Boats 94, 95 and 96

Built 1892–1895

Specification

Displacement tons	130
Dimensions	142¼pp x 15¼ x 8¼
Armament and Torpedo tubes as TB91	
Machinery	Triple expansion 200ihp
Speed	23 knots
Complement	18

Fate: TB94 and 95 were sold in 1919.

Loss: HM TB96 was in collision with SS *Tringa* off Gibraltar on 1 November 1915 .

Opposite: TB116. (Source not known)

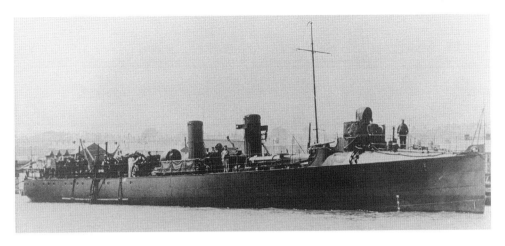

Torpedo Boats 114, 115, 116 and 117

Built 1902–1915

Specification

Displacement tons	219
Dimensions	165pp x 17½ x 6½
Armament	As TB109
Torpedo tubes	As TB109
Machinery	Triple expansion 3050ihp
Speed	25 knots
Complement	32

Fate: TBs 114 and 115 were broken up in 1919 and TB116 in 1921.

Loss: HM TB117 was in collision with the SS *Kamouraska* in the English Channel on 10 June 1917. She was later salvaged and became Dockyard Lighter C8 but was broken up in 1920.

First Class Torpedo Boats built by Yarrow & Co.

Torpedo Boat 14

Built 1878–1879

Specification

Displacement tons	33
Dimensions	86 x 11 x 4½
Torpedo tube	One 14in torpedo tube on the bow. Two reloads
Machinery	Compound engine giving 450ihp
Speed	21 knots

Fate: Broken up in 1904.

TB14. (Yarrow SB)

TB23. (Yarrow SB)

TB30. (Yarrow SB)

Torpedo Boats 17 and 18

Built 1878

Specification

Displacement tons	33
Dimensions	86 x 11 x 4½
Torpedo tube	One 14in with two reloads
Machinery	Compound engine giving 450ihp
Speed	21 knots
Complement	7

Note: Both these torpedo boats were under construction in England for the Imperial Russian Navy but were purchased by, and completed for, the Admiralty.

Fate: TB18 was based at Gibraltar and sold there in 1902 and TB17 was sold in 1907 at Malta.

Torpedo Boats 23 and 24

Built 1884–1886

Specification

Displacement tons	67
Dimensions	113½ x 12½ x 6¾
Armament	Two 3pdr
Torpedo tubes	Two 14in on the bow
Machinery	Compound engine giving 700ihp
Speed	20 knots
Complement	14

Note: Upon completion both were based at Malta and sold there in 1907.

Torpedo Boats 30, 31, 32, 33, 61, 62, 63, 64, 65, 66, 67, 69, 70, 71, 72, 73, 74, 75, 76 and 77

Built 1885–1887

Specifications

Displacement tons	60
Dimensions	125¼ x 13 x 5½
Armament	Two 3pdr
Torpedo tubes	Five 14in
Machinery	Triple expansion, 670ihp
Speed	19½ knots
Complement	16

Note: The bows of this group did not have to be rebuilt to produce a straight stem (see above).

Fate: TBs 30, 31, 32, 61, 62 and 63 were broken up prior to the First World War. The remainder, with the exception of TB64 and 75, were broken up between 1919 and 1923.

Losses: HM TB64 on 23 March 1915 was wrecked in the Aegean Sea. HM TB75 on 8 August 1892 was in collision while off the Maidens with HM TB77, and later sank.

Torpedo Boat 79

Built 1886

Specification

Displacement tons	75
Dimensions	128¾ x 13 x 5½
Armament	Two 3pdr
Torpedo tubes	Five 14in
Machinery	Triple expansion of 1,000ihp
Speed	22¾ knots
Complement	16

Note: HM TB79 was one of the earlier TBs to be powered by triple expansion engines and had two funnels. Early in her career she was commanded by Prince George (who later became King George V).

TB79. (Yarrow S.B.)

Torpedo Boats 39 and 40

Built 1882–1885

Specification

Displacement tons	40
Dimensions	100pp x 12½ x 4
Armament	Two 1in twin Nordenfelt
Torpedo tube	One 14in
Machinery	Triple expansion, 500ihp
Speed	20 knots
Complement	15

Note: Both these Torpedo Boats were built in England for the Chilean Navy and had already reached that country, when, in 1885, the Russian war scare of 1885 occurred, and the Admiralty purchased them. They sailed to reinforce our Pacific Squadron based at British Columbia. In Canada they received the unofficial names of *Swift* and *Sure*.

Fate: Both were scrapped in 1905.

Torpedo Boat 80

Built 1886–1887

Specification

Displacement tons	105
Dimensions	135pp x 14 x 6
Armament	Three 3pdr
Torpedo tubes	One bow tube and two trainable, all 14in
Machinery	Triple expansion 1,540ihp
Speed	23 knots
Complement	21

Note: This was the first Torpedo Boat to have a 'turtle back' forecastle for better seaworthiness.

Fate: Broken up in 1921.

Torpedo Boats 82, 83, 84, 85, 86 and 87

Built 1884

Specification

Displacement tons	105
Dimensions	142pp x 13¾ x 5¾
Armament	Three 3pdr
Torpedo tubes	Three 14in

Machinery	Triple expansion 1,800ihp
Speed	23 knots
Complement	19

Note: Very similar design to TB79 but with a 'turtle back' forecastle.

Fate: All sold between 1919 and 1921, excepting TB8.

Loss: HM TB84 sank off Malta after colliding with HMS *Ardent* (Destroyer) in 1906.

TB80. (Yarrow SB)

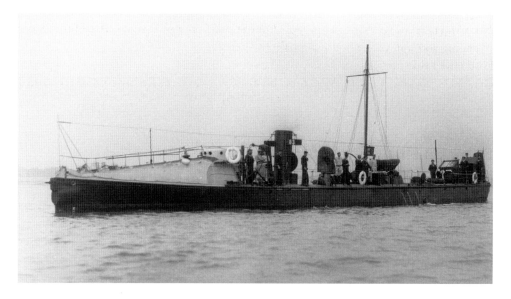

TB83. (Imperial War Museum)

Toroedo Boats 88 and 89

Built 1892–1894

Specification

Displacement tons	105
Dimensions	142pp x 14¾ x 7½
Armament	Three 3pdr
Torpedo tubes	Three 18in, one bow, two deck
Machinery	Triple expansion, 1,850ihp
Speed	23 knots
Complement	18

Note: Designed as an improvement on the TB39 group.
Fate: Both broken up in 1919.

Torpedo Boat 90

Built 1892–1895

Specification

Displacement tons	105
Dimensions	104¼ x 14½ x 6½
Armament and Torpedo tube as TB88	
Machinery	Triple expansion 1,500ihp
Speed	23 knots
Complement	18

Note: Intended to be a repeat order of TB88 but building was delayed and a four-cylinder engine and water tube boiler were fitted for trials.
Loss: HM TB90 capsized off Gibraltar on 25 April 1918.
General Note: The majority of Torpedo Boats were re-engined, re-boilered and re-armed at least once in their service career.

Ex-Indian First Class Torpedo Boats

Torpedo Boats 100 (ex-*Baluchi*), 102 (ex-*Karen*) and 103 (ex-*Pathan*)

Built 1887–1888 by J.I. Thornycroft & Co.

Specification

Displacement tons	96
Dimensions	134½ x 14¾ x 7
Armament	Two 1in twin Nordenfelt or two 3pdr
Torpedo tubes	Five 14in

Machinery	Triple expansion giving 1,260ihp
Speed	23 knots
Complement	18

Note: Three of seven ex-Indian Torpedo Boats built in England by order of the India Office but taken over by the Royal Navy.

Fate: All believed to have been broken up in 1909.

Torpedo Boat 101 (ex-*Ghurka*)

Built 1887–1888 by Hanna Donald & Wilson

Specification

Displacement tons	92
Dimensions	135 x 14 x 7
Armament	As TB100
Torpedo tubes	As TB100
Machinery	Triple expansion giving 1,000ihp
Speed	21½ knots
Complement	18

Note: As TB100, but one of seven.

Fate: Broken up in 1920.

Torpedo Boats 104 (ex-*Maharatta*), 105 (ex-*Sikh*) and 106 (ex-*Rajput*)

Built 1889 by J.S. White & Co.

Specification

Displacement tons	95
Dimensions	135 x 14½ x 7½
Armament	As TB100
Torpedo tubes	As TB100
Machinery	Triple expansion giving 1,000ihp
Speed	22 knots
Complement	18

Note: As TB100 but three of seven.

Fate: TB106 was broken up in 1910 and TBs 104 and 105 in 1920.

First Class Torpedo Boats by other builders

Torpedo Boat 97

Built 1892–1894 by Laird Bros

Specification

Displacement tons	130
Dimensions	140½ x 16 x 7½
Armament	Three 3pdr
Torpedo tubes	Three 18in single tubes
Machinery	Triple expansion giving 2,000ihp
Speed	23 knots
Complement	18

Note: The first and only Torpedo Boat built by Laird's, who concentrated on Torpedo Catchers and Torpedo Boat Destroyers.

Fate: Sold in 1920 at Gibraltar where she mostly served.

Torpedo Boat 15

Built 1879 by Hanna Donald & Wilson

Specification

Displacement tons	28
Dimensions	87 x 10¼ x 5½
Torpedo tube	One 14in with two reloads
Machinery	One compound engine to one shaft 450ihp
Speed	21 knots
Complement	15

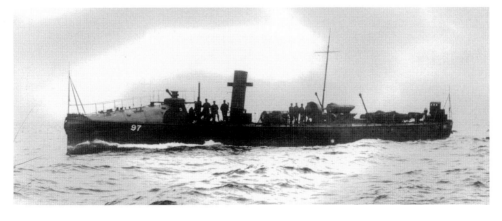

TB97. (Cammell Laird)

Note: Apart from TB101 was the only TB by this firm.

Fate: Served at the Cape and decommissioned before 1904. Torpedo Boat 16 was ordered from Lewin of Poole but cancelled about 1880 due to construction delays.

Torpedo Boat 13

Built 1878 by Maudslay of Lambeth

Specification

Displacement tons	28
Dimensions	87 x 10¾ x 4
Torpedo tube	One 14in with two reloads
Machinery	Compound engine to one shaft 450ihp
Speed	20 knots
Complement	15

Note: TB13 is reported as being built with a brass hull.

Fate: Sold 1905.

Torpedo Boat 20

Built 1880 by Rennie of Greenwich

Specification

Displacement tons	28
Dimensions	87 x 10 x 4
Torpedo tube	One 14in with two reloads
Machinery	Compound engine to one shaft 360ihp
Speed	16½ knots
Complement	15

General Note: Torpedo Boats 13 to 20 later in their life had the torpedo tube removed and two torpedo carriers fitted, the reverse of TB1.

Fate: TB20 largely served at Hong Kong and was sold in 1905.

Second Class Torpedo Boats

Second class torpedo boats were built between 1878 and 1889 but were never as efficient as the first class design. The second class boats were smaller and intended to be carried in falls at the davits of seagoing naval vessels to be launched as required or for action and recovered, after same using the carrier vessel as a base. The Admiralty were quite impressed with the idea and designed, built and commissioned HMS *Vulcan* as a Torpedo Boat Carrier.

HMS *Vulcan* was also described as a Depot Ship Cruiser and displaced 6,620 tons, built by HM Dockyard, Portsmouth commissioning in 1889. She had a length of 350ft and a beam of 58ft and was armed with eight 4.7in and twelve 3pdr guns, being renamed *Defiance III* in 1931. Another Torpedo Carrier was HMS *Hecla*, a conversion from the mercantile SS *British Crown*.

Torpedo Boat 63

Built 1878 by Herreschoff of the USA

Specification

Displacement tons	15
Dimensions	60 x 7½ x 3
Torpedo tubes (intended)	Two 14in
Machinery	See Note
Speed	16 knots
Complement	7

Vulcan.
(National
Maritime
Museum)

TB63.
(Source not
known)

Note: TB63 was purchased as an experimental craft for trials of her unusual coil boiler which, although temperamental, was very efficient for steam raising. She was constructed with a timber hull and steel structure.

Fate: Not known.

Torpedo Boats 51, 52, 53, 54, 55, 56, 57, 58, 59, 60, 61 and 62

Built 1878–1879 by J.I. Thornycroft & Co.

Specification

Displacement tons	10½
Dimensions	60½ x 7½ x 3
Torpedo armament	Two 14in torpedoes in lowering cages
Machinery	One compound engine to one shaft giving between 120 and 150ihp
Speed	15/16 knots
Complement	7

Note: Of very light construction and not suitable for heavy seas.

Fate: Broken up 1902.

Torpedo Boats 64, 65, 66, 67, 68, 69, 70, 71, 72 and 73

Built 1880–1881 by J.I. Thornycroft & Co.

Specification

Displacement tons	13
Dimensions	63 x 7¾ x 3½
Torpedo armament	Two 14in torpedoes in dropping gear
Machinery	Compound engine of 110ihp
Speed	16½ knots
Complement	7

Note: Again, very lightly built TBs even so HM TB68 was deployed to Newfoundland.

Fate: All broken up in 1902.

Torpedo Boats 76, 77, 78, 82, 85, 82, 85, 86, 87, 88, 89, 90, 91, 92 and 95

Built 1880–1883 by J.I. Thornycroft

Specification

Displacement tons	12½
Dimensions	63pp x 7½ x 3½
Torpedo tubes	Two 14in at the bow
Machinery	Compound engine of 170ihp

TB51. (Source not known)

TB62. (Source not known)

Speed	16½ knots
Complement	7

Note: HM TBs 76 and 77 were built with the coil boiler (see TB63 above).
Fate: All broken up 1902.

Torpedo Boat 98

Built 1880–1883 by J.I. Thornycroft & Co.

Specification

Displacement tons	14½
Dimensions	66½wl x 7½ x 2¾
Torpedo tubes	Provision for Two 14in on the bow
Machinery	A Ruthven Water Turbine jet giving 167ihp
Speed	11 knots
Complement	7

Propulsion note: Built to explore the feasibility of the above system of water jet propulsion but the speed was low, steering difficult and the out fall very noisy.
Fate: Broken up in 1902.

Torpedo Boats 99 and 100

Built 1884–1886 by J.I. Thornycroft & Co.

Specification

Displacement tons	12
Dimensions	65 x 8 x 3½
Torpedo tubes	Two 14in fixed
Machinery	Compound engine giving 190ihp
Speed	16½ knots
Complement	7

Note: Both built with a semi-tunnel stern and twin rudders.
Fate: Broken up 1902.

Torpedo Boats 1, 2, 3, 4, 5, 6, 7, 8, 9, 10, 11 and 12

Built 1883–1888 by White & Co.

Specification

Displacement tons	10½ to 14
Dimensions	56 x 9½ x 4¾ or thereabouts
Armament	1 or 2mg
Torpedo armament	Two 14in torpedoes on dropping gear OR one 14in torpedo tube
Machinery	Engines of 140 to 200ihp
Speed	Average of 15 knots
Complement	9

Note: Constructed of wood with cut away sterns.
Fates: TB2 sold 1900, 1, 3, 4, 7, 8 and 10 sold 1905, 5 sold 1909, 6 sold 1907, 9 and 11 sold 1912 and 12 sold 1910.

Torpedo Boats 74, 75, 96 and 97

Built 1881–1883 by Yarrow & Co.

Specification

Displacement tons	12
Dimensions	63pp x 7½ x 3½
Armament	1 mg
Torpedo tubes	Two 14in on the bow
Machinery	Compound engine of 220ihp
Speed	16 knots

Note: Similar to TB64.
Fate: All sold 1902.

Torpedo Boats 49 and 50

Built 1888 by Yarrow & Co.

Specification	HM TB49	HM TB50
Displacement tons	15	15½
Dimensions	59½ x 8¼ x 3	60 x 8½ x 3
Armament	One Nordenfelt mg	
Torpedo tube	One 14in	
Machinery	200ihp	
Speed	16½ knots	
Complement	9	

Fate: Sold in 1902.

TB50. (Yarrow SB)

HM Torpedo Boats 39, 40, 41, 42, 43, 44, 45, 46, 47 and 48

Built 1889 by Yarrow & Co.

Specification

Displacement tons	16½
Dimensions	60 x 9¼ x 4½
Armament	One mg
Torpedo Armament	Two 14in torpedoes in dropping gear
Machinery	Compound engine of 240ihp
Speed	16½ knots
Complement	9

Note: These were the last second class Torpedo Boats built for the Royal Navy and six of this group were carried on board HMS *Vulcan* (see page 55).

Fate: All sold 1902 or later.

Chapter 3

Motor Launches and Coastal Motor Boats

Ex-American/Canadian Motor Launches 75ft and 80ft (MLs)

Builder	Electric Boat Co.	Canadian Vickers
Motor Launch Nos	1 to 50 inc.	51 to 550 and 551 to 580 inc.

Specification

Displacement tons	34	37
Dimensions	75 x 12 x 4	80 x 12¾ x 4
Armament	One 13pdr or one 3pdr	One 3in
	1 or 2mg	1 or 2mg
Machinery	Petrol engines	Petrol engines
	440hp to two shafts	440hp to two shafts
Anti-submarine	Depth charges were carried	Depth charges were carried
Range	1,000nm at 15 knots	
Speed	18–20 knots	
Complement	8	10

Note: The Motor Launch was a new type of craft for the Royal Navy and was used for many varied tasks including inshore minesweeping, coastal mine laying, hydrophone vessels, smokescreen generators and anti-submarine tasks. The evolution of the ML was as a direct result of the great success resulting from the patrols of requisitioned Motor Boats which had been formed into the Motor Boat Reserve, and were mainly craft of ex-private ownership varying from 3 to 75 tons displacement and armed according to capacity. The first fifty MLs were ordered from Elco in the United States with a length of 75ft with further orders for 530 launches of 80ft length from Canadian Vickers. They were too small for transatlantic delivery and so crossed to the UK on merchant ships as deck cargo.

Losses: HM ML19 caught fire at Harwich on 31 January 1916.
  HM ML4 caught fire on 18 May 1916 whilst making way in the Suez Canal.
  HM ML149 was destroyed by fire at Taranto on 10 September 1916.
  HM MLs 230, 253 and 255 were deck cargo on the freighter *Inverbie*, which on 14 September 1916 was torpedoed in the Gulf of Squillace.
  HM ML197 was wrecked near Ballincourty Lighthouse on 31 January 1917.
  HM ML534 was destroyed by fire at Taranto on 13 April 1917.
  HM ML431 was destroyed by fire at Poole on 22 April 1917.
  HM MLs 540 and 541 were deck cargo on the freighter *Hunstrick*, when it was torpedoed on 8 June 1917, off Tangier.

ML6. (Imperial War Museum)

ML260. (Imperial War Museum)

HM ML474 was shelled on 23 July 1917 near Chios.

HM ML52 was destroyed by fire in Sandown Bay on 29 November 1917.

HM ML278 was wrecked on Dunkirk Pier on 15 January 1918.

HM ML55 was destroyed by fire in a shipyard at Sittingbourne while undergoing refit on 28 January 1918.

HM ML421 was wrecked in Seaford Bay on 6 April 1918.

HM ML356 was in collision with an unknown vessel off Dover on 11 April 1918.

HM MLs 110 and 424 were lost in action at Zeebrugge on that St George's Day, 23 April 1918.

HM ML254 was sunk by own forces while off Ostend to avoid her falling into the hands of the enemy on 10 May 1918.

HM ML64 was destroyed by fire in Granton Harbour on 10 June 1918.

HM ML403 contacted the pistol and blew up while endeavouring to salvage a floating German torpedo in Runswick Bay.

HM ML247 was wrecked off St Ives on 29 September 1918.

HM ML561 was mined on 21 October 1918 off Ostend.

HM MLs 18, 62 and 191 were lost on 29 September 1919 due to heavy weather off the Norwegian coast.

HM ML98 was lost – date, cause and place unknown.

HM ML121 was in collision with another vessel on 22 December 1918 off the Seine Bank.

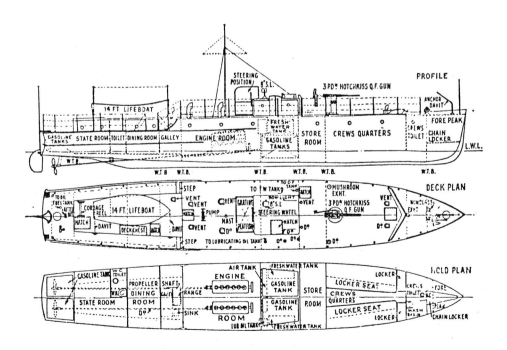

Outline of 80ft ML First World War.

HM ML152 took the ground on 2 January 1920 off Southern Oland.

HM ML196 caught fire – date and place unknown.

HM ML434 caught fire on the Danube – date and cause unknown.

HM ML521 caught fire at Portsmouth – date and cause unknown.

HM ML566 sank in heavy weather on 22 December 1918 off Cape Barfleur.

HM MLs 97, 127 and 229 became constructive total losses – dates, causes and places unknown.

Note: That so many MLs should be lost by fire deserves a comment regarding their fuel. This of course was petrol and at any time was very dangerous. Presumably and in consequence thereof, 'brew ups' were not uncommon. It is surprising that only two MLs were lost by mining but the shallow draught of these craft should be remembered.

The Thornycroft 70ft Coastal Motor Boat Minelayers are not listed herein but are included in *Mine Warfare Vessels of the Royal Navy 1908–to Date*, by the same author.

Thornycroft Coastal Motor Boats 40ft (CMB)

Coastal Motor Boat 1, 2, 3, 4, 5, 6, 7, 8, 9, 10, 13, 40, 41, 42, 47, 48, 50, 55, 56, 112, 121, 122 and 123 built by J.I. Thornycroft & Co.

CMBs 1–13 inclusive built 1916

CMBs 40–56 inclusive built 1918

CMB112 built 1919, and 121–123 1921

CMBs 11 and 12 built by T. Bunn in 1916

CMB 43 and 49 built by Taylor & Bates in 1918

CMBs 44, 45 and 59 built by J.W. Bros in 1918

CMBs 46, 53 and 54 built by F. Maynard in 1918

CMBs 51, 52, 60 and 61 built by Salter Bros in 1918

CMBs 57 and 58 built by Wills & Packham in 1918

Specification

Displacement tons	5
Dimensions	40pp x 8½ x 2½/3
Arxnanient	2/4mg.
Torpedo armament	One 18in in trough.
Machinery	One petrol engine – Thornycroft V8 or V12 giving 250bhp, 25 knots
	OR Fiat 275bhp, 35 knots
	OR Green 12 giving 275bhp
	and an uprated Thornycroft V12 for CMB112, 38 knots.
Complement	3

Losses: HM CMB1 on 19 June 1917 in a surface action off Ostend.

HM CMB2 on 9 July 1918 caught fire at Portsmouth.

HM CMB8 on 27 September 1917 sunk by own forces to avoid capture off the Belgian coast.

CMB 40ft. (Imperial War Museum)

HM CMB10 on 7 May 1918 caught fire at Dover.

HM CMB40 on 11 August 1918 by enemy aircraft off Terschelling.

HM CMB42 on 11 August 1918 by enemy aircraft at Terschelling.

HM CMB47 on 11 August 1918 by enemy aircraft off Terschelling.

HM CMB50 scuttled by own forces on 19 July 1918 off Heligoland.

HM CMB11 on 2 November 1917 was in collision and caught fire off Dover.

Thornycroft Coastal Motor Boats 55ft (CMB)

CMBs 14A, 15A, 16A, 17A, 18A and 21B built by J.I. Thornycroft in 1917

CMBs 24A, 25BB, 26B, 27A, 29A, 31BB, 33A, 34A. 36A, 65A, 75A, 78E, 80C, 82C, 83CE, 87B, 93E, 94E, 95E, 96E and 97E. 118CK and 120F (the latter three were not completed) built by J.I. Thornycroft in 1918

CMBs 19A, 68B, 73B, 74B, 84C and 86BD built by Taylor & Bates in 1918

CMBs 114D and 115DE built by Taylor & Bates in 1919

CMBs 20A, 37A, 39B, 69A, 70A, 72A, 75B, 77A, 79A and 81C built by Casper & Nicholson in 1918

CMBs 98ED and 99ED built by Camper & Nicholson in 1919

CMBs 118D and 119D built by Camper & Nicholson in 1920

CMBs 22B, 30B, 63BD and 64BD built by Wills & Packham in 1918

CMBs 116D and 117D built by Wills & Packham in 1919

CMBs 23B, 62BB and 67A built by Salter Bros in 1918

CMB 55ft. (Imperial War Museum)

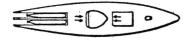

CMB 55ft 1915.

CMBs 29A and 35A built by Rowhedge Iron Works in 1918

CMBs 90BD, 91BD and 92BD built by Rowhedge Iron Works in 1919

CMBs 32A, 38B, 66BB and 71A built by F. Maynard in 1918

CMBs 85C and 88BD built by F. Maynard in 1919

CMB 89BD builder not known

Specification

Displacement tons	11
Dimensions	55pp x 11 x 3
Armament	Four mg AA. Four depth charges
Torpedo armament	One or two 18in in troughs. If these craft were used for mine-laying, neither torpedoes nor depth charges were carried
Machinery	Two petrol engines to two shafts (see machinery note below)
Complement	3/5

Machinery Note: The letter codes after the number of the Coastal Motor Boat gave a visual indication of the make of the engine which propelled that particular boat:

Engine Type & No., Bhp, Speed and Torpedo Capacity.

A   Two Thornycroft V12 each 250bhp, 35 knots – 1 torpedo

B   Two Green 12 each 275bhp, 37 knots – 1 torpedo

C   Two Sunbeam each 450bhp, 41 knots – 1 torpedo

D   Two Green 18 each 450bhp – 1 torpedo

E   Two Thornycroft Y12 each 350bhp, 41 knots – 1 torpedo

F   Two Not known – 1 torpedo

BD   Two Green 12 each 275bhp, 35 knots – 2 torpedoes

CE   Two Not known – 2 torpedoes

CK   Two Not known – 2 torpedoes

DE   Two Green 18 each 450bhp, 40 knots – 2 torpedoes

ED   Two Thornycroft Y12 each 350bhp – 2 torpedoes

Losses: HM CMB18A on 12 April 1918 was in collision off the Belgian coast.

HM CMB24A on 18 August 1919 in the attack on the Bolshevik Naval Base at Kronstadt.

HM CMB33A sank on 12 April 1918 in a surface action off Ostend.

HM CMB82C in 1923 sank while on passage to Portsmouth.

HM CMB114D in April 1923 caught fire off the Nab and sank.

HM CMB39B on 28 April 1918 caught fire at Dunkirk.

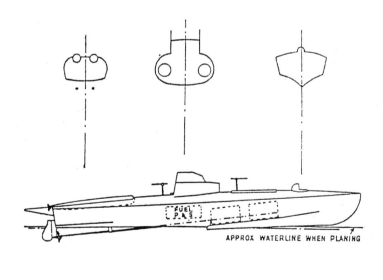

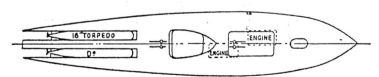

Outline of CMB 55ft.

HM CMB79A was lost on 18 September 1919 in the attack on the Bolshevik Naval Base at Kronstadt.

HM CMB99ED caught fire at Portsmouth in 1920.

HM CMB62BD was lost on 18 September 1919 in the attack on the Bolshevik Naval Base at Kronstadt. Likewise HM CMB67A.

HM CMB90BD was sunk as a target in 1923.

HM CMB71A missing on 15 October 1918, possibly foundered after collision off the Belgian coast.

Ex-Greek Motor Launches

Motor Launches *Mimi* and *Tou-Tou*

Built 1915

Specification from J.I. Thornycroft's Yard List

Name	Mimi	Tou-Tou
Yard No.	750	782
Type	Fast Launch	Launch
Length & Beam	40 x 8	40 x 8
Thornycroft Engine	128hp	120hp
Speed on trials	14 knots	16¾ knots
Armament	Nil but both fitted with a 3pdr Hotchkiss piece and a Maxim mg	

Mimi and Tou-Tou. (Vosper Thornycroft)

Note: Both under construction in England as seaplane tenders for the Royal Greek Air
Service but taken over by the Admiralty for the expedition to Lake Tanganyika to
engage the armed German lake steamers which were in undisputed command of the
lake.

Both HMS *Mimi* and *Tou-Tou* were transported the 8,000 miles to the lake with
a supporting naval party and assistance from the Belgian armed forces. The Germans
had three armed steamers and on 26 December 1915 the British Tanganyika Squadron
comprising HMS *Mimi* and HMS *Tou-Tou*, on the report of enemy in sight, sailed
from their newly built harbour of Kalemie to engage the German armed steamer
Kingani. The action was successful and *Kingani* surrendered to the British squadron. As
the weather was bad, *Kingani* was ordered to make for Kalemie where she filled with
water as a result of gunfire received, and sank to the bottom of the lake. In three days,
however, she had been repaired and refloated and armed with a Belgian 12pdr and
commissioned as HMS *Fifi*.

The second engagement took place on 9 February 1916 when the enemy in sight
was identified as the German armed steamer *Hedwig von Wissmann*. HMS *Fifi* opened
fire at 7,500 yards, the range rapidly closed, and HMS *Mimi* then engaged at 3,800
yards. Again the enemy abandoned ship, with the *Hedwig von Wissmann* on fire before
she sank. Remaining were the German unarmed fast launch *Wami*, which, when aware
of the RN ships, ran on shore and was set on fire by her commander. The larger (200ft
in length and steel built) *Graf von Gotson*, armed with two 4in guns and two smaller,
was blown up by her commander in the German lake port of Kigoma.

So was Central Africa cleared of German naval forces and prestige.

Loss: HMS *Tou-Tou* was lost in heavy weather after the first engagement in Lake
Tanganyika.

HMS *Fifi* (ex-*Kingani*) was 55ft in length and armed with a 37mm gun, speed
7 knots when captured.

Note: Detailed information kindly supplied by the Naval Historical Library MOD (N)
London, of which a précis is given above.

Chapter 4

Torpedo Catchers

HMS *Rattlesnake* Torpedo Catcher

HMS	Commenced	Completed	Builder
Rattlesnake	1885	1887	Laird

Specification

Displacement tons	550
Dimensions	200pp x 23x 10½
Armament	One 4in QF, six 3pdr QF
Torpedo tubes	Four 14in with four reloads
Machinery	Triple expansion all giving 2,700ihp to two shafts
Speed	19½ knots
Complement	66

Note: HMS *Rattlesnake* was a one-ship class of a new type designed for catching Torpedo Boats. With her gun armament and torpedoes she should have been a match for any such vessel within range. The Admiralty decided that *Rattlesnake* was of sufficient performance to justify that further ships of this type be laid down. In consequence the 'Grasshopper', 'Sharpshooter', 'Alarm' and 'Hazard' Classes of Torpedo Catcher were laid down over the next ten years.

Construction note: HMS *Rattlesnake* was not armoured but she did have a semi-protective steel deck.

Fate: *Rattlesnake* was sold for breaking up in 1910.

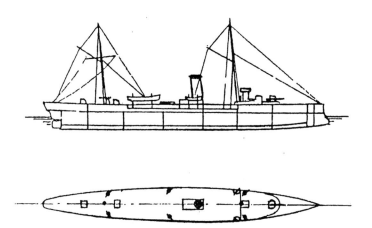

Rattlesnake, 1886.

Rattlesnake. (Cammell Laird)

'Grasshopper' Class Torpedo Catchers

HMS	Commenced	Completed	Builder
Grasshopper	1886	1888	HM Dockyard, Sheerness
Sandfly	1886	1888	HM Dockyard, Devonport
Spider	1886	1888	HM Dockyard, Devonport

Specification

Displacement tons	526
Dimensions	200pp x 23 x 10½
Armament	One 4in QF, six 3pdr QF
Torpedo tubes	Four 14in with four reloads
Machinery	Triple expansion all giving 2,700ihp to two shafts
Speed	19½ knots
Complement	66

Note: These three ships were very similar to *Rattlesnake* but of slightly less tonnage. They had quite a short career with the Fleet with *Spider* being sold in 1903 and *Grasshopper* and *Sandfly* sold for breaking up in 1905.

'Sharpshooter' Class Torpedo Catchers

HMS	Commenced	Completed	Builder
Gleaner	1889	1891	HM Dockyard, Sheerness
Gossamer	1889	1891	HM Dockyard, Sheerness
Salamander	1888	1891	HM Dockyard, Chatham
Seagull	1888	1891	HM Dockyard, Chatham
Sharpshooter	1888	1889	HM Dockyard, Devonport

Gossamer. (Source
not known)

Spanker. (Imperial
War Museum)

Sheldrake	1888	1890	HM Dockyard, Chatham
Skipjack	1888	1891	HM Dockyard, Chatham
Spanker	1888	1890	HM Dockyard, Devonport
Speedwell	1888	1890	HM Dockyard, Devonport

Specification

Displacement tons	735
Dimensions	230pp x 27 x 10½
Armament	Two 4.7in QF in single mountings at 'A' and 'Y' positions. Four 3pdr QF
Torpedo tubes	Five 14in tubes
Machinery	Triple expansion, 3,500hp to two shafts
Speed	18 knots
Complement	90

Note: The 'Sharpshooter' Class were very well built and individual ships were even deployed as cruisers from time to time.

Weapon note: With this class the 4.7in guns gave them a harder hitting armament than the 'Grasshopper', it having been found that the 4.7in gun was superior in all respects to the 4in.

Fate: *Gleaner* sold 1905, *Gossamer* 1920, *Salamander* sold relegated to harbour service in 1904, *Sheldrake* broken up in 1907, *Spanker* and *Speedwell* broken up in 1920.

Loss: HMS *Seagull* on 30 September 1918 sank after being in collision with the SS *Corrib* in the river Clyde.

'Alarm' Class Torpedo Catchers

HMS	Commenced	Completed	Builder
Alarm	1891	1894	HM Dockyard, Sheerness
Antelope	1889	1894	HM Dockyard, Devonport
Circe	1890	1893	HM Dockyard, Sheerness
Hebe	1890	1894	HM Dockyard, Sheerness
Jaseur	1891	1893	Naval Construction & Armament Co. (Vickers)
Jason	1891	1893	Vickers
Leda	1891	1893	HM Dockyard, Sheerness
Niger	1891	1893	Vickers
Onyx	1891	1894	Laird
Renard	1891	1894	Laird
Speedy	1892	1894	Thornycroft

Specification

Displacement tons	810
Dimensions	230 x 27 x 12½

Niger. (Vickers SB&E)

Speedy. (Imperial War Museum)

Armament	Two 4.7in in single mountings in 'A' and 'Y' positions, four 4pdr QF, one mg
Torpedo tubes	Five 14in tubes, excepting *Jaseur, Jason, Niger, Onyx* and *Speedy* which had three 18in
Machinery	Triple expansion, 3,500hp to two shafts
Speed	18 knots
Fuel	100–160 tons coal
Complement	85

Identification note: HMS *Speedy* had three funnels, the remainder of the class having two.

Note: These torpedo catchers were the most successful of the four classes that were built, particularly HMS *Speedy*, which was the first of this type to be built by Thornycroft and was fitted with that firm's water tube boilers, which were most reliable.

Fate: *Alarm* was sold in 1907, *Antelope* relegated to harbour service in 1914, *Circe* broken up 1920, *Hebe* converted to a Submarine Depot Ship in 1910, *Jaseur* sold 1905, *Leda* broken up 1922, *Onyx* converted to a Submarine Depot Ship in 1907 and *Renard* sold in 1905.

Losses: HMS *Jason* on 7 April 1917 was mined off the west coast of Scotland.
HMS *Niger* on 11 November 1914 whilst off Deal was torpedoed by U-12.
HMS *Speedy* on 3 September 1914 was mined in the river Humber.

'Hazard' Class Torpedo Catchers

HMS	Commenced	Completed	Builder
Dryad (later *Hamadryad*)	1893	1894	HM Dockyard, Chatham
Halcyon	1893	1895	HM Dockyard, Devonport
Harrier	1893	1895	HM Dockyard, Devonport
Hazard	1892	1894	HM Dockyard, Pembroke
Hussar	1893	1895	HM Dockyard, Devonport

Specification

Displacement tons	1,070
Dimensions	250pp x 33½ x 11½
Armament	Two 4.7in single in 'A' and 'Y' positions, four 6pdr, one Nordenfelt 5-barrelled mg
Torpedo tubes	Five 18in with two reloads
Machinery	Triple expansion 3,500hp to two shafts
Speed	18½ knots
Fuel	100/160 tons coal
Complement	120

Note: These were rather unusual looking vessels with the fore funnel at the break of the forecastle and the second funnel at the break of the poop which gave them a shelter deck stern.

Fates: *Dryad* and *Harrier* were broken up in 1920 and *Hussar* in 1921. *Halcyon* and *Hazard* were converted to Depot Ships in 1915.

Loss: HMS *Hazard* was in collision with an unknown vessel in the English Channel on 28 January 1918.

Halcyon. (Imperial War Museum)

Chapter 5

Coastal Destroyers

'Insect' Class Coastal Destroyers

HMS	Launches	Builder
Cricket (later TB1)	1906	White
Dragonfly (later TB2)	1906	White
Firefly (later TB3)	1906	White
Sandfly (later TB4)	1906	White
Spider (later TB5)	1906	White
Gadfly (later TB6)	1906	Thornycroft
Glowworm (later TB7)	1906	Thornycroft
Gnat (later TB8)	1906	Thornycroft
Grasshopper (later TB9)	1907	Thornycroft
Greenfly (later TB10)	1907	Thornycroft
Mayfly (later TB11)	1907	Yarrow SB
Moth (later TB12)	1907	Yarrow SB

Specification

	TBs 1, 2, 3, 4 and 5	TBs 6, 7, 8, 9 and 10	TBs 11 and 12
Displacement tons	235/261	244/255	256/283
Dimensions	175 x 17½ x 6	166½ x 17½ x 6	172 x 18 x 6
Armament	Two 12pdr	One 12pdr	One 12pdr
Torpedo tubes	Three 18in	Three 18in	Three 18in
Machinery	Turbines 3,750shp to three shafts		
Speed	25½ knots		
Complement	33		

Note: All served in the North Sea and the Dover Patrol.

Fate: The remaining TBs of this class were sold for breaking up between 1920 and 1921.

Losses: HM TB4, while in tow for breaking up, went aground off Westward Ho on 11 January 1921.

HM TB9 was in collision in the North Sea on 26 July 1916.

HM TB10 was mined in the North Sea on 10 June 1915.

HM TB11 was mined in the North Sea on 7 March 1916.

HM TB12 was mined in the North Sea on 10 June 1915.

Gadfly. (R. Perkins)

'TB13' Class Coastal Destroyers

HMS	Launched	Builder
TB13	1907	White
TB14	1907	White
TB15	1907	White
TB16	1907	White
TB17	1907	Denny
TB18	1908	Denny
TB19	1907	Thornycroft
TB20	1908	Thornycroft
TB21	1907	Hawthorne Leslie
TB22	1908	Hawthorne Leslie
TB23	1907	Yarrow
TB24	1908	Palmer
TB25	1908	White
TB26	1908	White
TB27	1908	White
TB28	1908	White
TB29	1908	Denny
TB30	1908	Denny
TB31	1908	Thornycroft
TB32	1908	Thornycroft

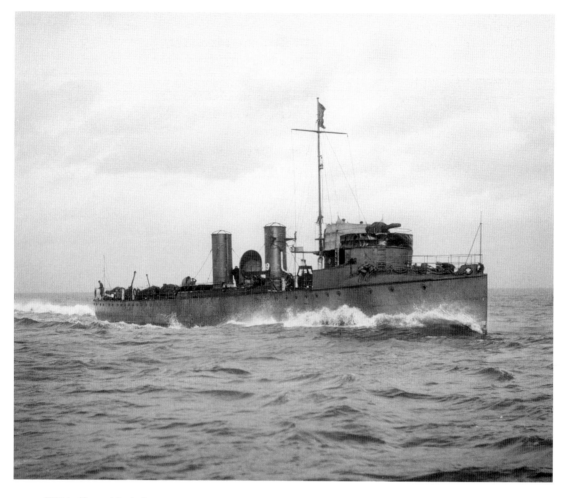

TB21. (Swan Hunter)

TB33	1909	Hawthorne Leslie
TB34	1909	Hawthorne Leslie
TB35	1909	Palmer
TB36	1909	Palmer

Specification Group 1
TBs 13, 14, 15, 16, 25, 26, 27 and 28   Displacement tons 256/283
Dimensions 182 x 18 x 6½

Specification Group 2
TBs 17, 18, 29 and 30   Displacement tons 259/272
Dimensions 180 x 18 x 6½

Specification Group 3
TBs 19, 20, 31 and 32   Displacement tons 278/312
Dimensions 178¾ x 18¼ x 6½

Specification Group 4

TBs 21, 22, 33 and 34

Displacement tons 308/328

Dimensions 185 x 18¾ x 6½

Specification Group 5

TB23

Displacement tons 263/282

Dimensions 177½ x 18 x 6½

Specification Group 6

TBs 24, 35, and 36

Displacement tons 292/315

Dimensions 177 x 17¾ x 6½

All TBs

Armament	Two 12pdr (3in)
Torpedo tubes	Three 18in
Machinery	Turbines to three shafts, all giving 3,750/4,000shp
Speed	26/27 knots
Complement	33/35

Note: Each builder constructed to slightly different dimensions.

Fate: All sold between 1919 and 1923 except TBs 13 and 24.

Losses: HM TB13 sank after collision in the North Sea on 25 January 1916.

HM TB24 was wrecked off Dover harbour in bad weather on 19 March 1908.

Chapter 6

Coastal Escorts

'P' Class Coastal Escorts

HMS	Launched	Builder
P11	1915	White
P12	1915	White
P13 (ex-P17 and P75)	1916	Hamilton
P14	1916	Connell
P15	1916	Workman Clark
P16	1916	Workman Clark
P17 (II)	1915	Workman Clark
P18	1916	Inglis
P19	1916	Northumberland Shipbuilder
P20	1916	Northumberland Shipbuilder
P21	1916	Russell
P22	1916	Caird
P23	1916	Bartraxn
P24	1915	Harland & Wolff Govan
P25	1916	Harland & Wolff Govan
P26	1915	Tyne Iron Shipbuilders
P27	1915	Eltringham
P28	1916	R. Thompson
P29	1915	Gray
P30	1916	Gray
P31	1916	Readhead
P32	1916	Harkness
P33	1916	Napier & Miller
P34	1916	Barclay Curie
P35	1917	Caird
P36	1916	Eitringham
P37	1916	Gray
P38	1917	Hamilton
P39	1917	Inglis
P40	1916	White
P41	1917	Bartram
P45	1917	Gray
P46	1917	Ilarkmss
P47	1917	Readhead

P40. (Source not known)

P48	1917	Readhead
P49	1917	R. Thompson
P50	1916	Tyne Iron Shipbuilders
P52	1916	White
P53	1917	Barclay Curie
P54	1917	Barclay Curie
P57	1917	Hamilton
P58 (later *Spey*)	1918	Hamilton
P59	1917	White
P64	1917	Inglis

Specification

Displacement tons   613

Dimensions   244½ x 23¾ x 7½

Designed Armament Two 4in single

Actual Armament   One 4in single on a bandstand surmounting a deckhouse before the bridge, and a 2pdr pom-pom aft of the funnel. All of this class were additionally armed with two single 14in torpedo tubes, and two depth charge throwers were fitted.

Machinery   Steam turbines 3,500shp to two shafts giving 20 knots.

Fuel   50 tons oil fuel.

Complement   52

P50. (Imperial War Museum)

Notes: HMS P52 had two 4in single and one 2pdr single only. The 'P' Escorts were a splendid design that evolved from the torpedo boats of 1885 and later. The great advantages of the 'P' Escort's specification were good manoeuvrability, construction, shallow draft, and economy of fuel. Additionally, they were fitted with a hardened steel stem in the event of the need to ram a U-boat. It is understood that these were the best anti-submarine vessels of the First World War and suitable for all weathers.

Losses: HMS P12 on 4 November 1918 sank after collision with an unknown vessel in the English Channel.

HMS P26 on 10 April 1917 struck a mine and sank whilst on anti-submarine patrol off Le Havre.

'Kingfisher' Class Coastal Escorts

HMS	Launched	Builder
Kingfisher	1935	Fairfield
Mallard	1936	Stephen
Puffin	1936	Stephen
Kittiwake	I 936	Thornycroft
Sheldrake	1937	Thorrrjcroft
Widgeon	1938	Yarrow
Guillemott	1939	Denny
Pintail	1939	Denny
Shearwater	1939	White

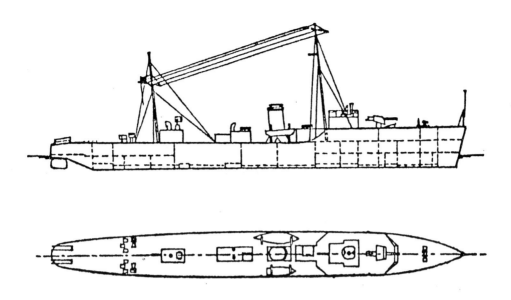

'Kingfisher' Class 1935.

Kittiwake. (Imperial War Museum)

Specification

	Kingfisher Mallard Puffin	Kittiwake Sheldrake Widgeon	Guillemot Pintail Shearwater
Displacement tons	510	530	580
Dimensions	243¼ x 26½ x 6	243¼ x 26½ x 6½	243¼ x 25½ x 7¼
Armament (All)	One 4in DP, two 20mm AA, four 0.5in mg AA		
Anti-Submarine	Two depth charge racks and throwers		
Machinery	Two shaft geared turbines all giving 3,600shp		
Speed	20 knots		
Fuel	160 tons oil fuel		
Complement	60		

Class note: This class of patrol vessel had a destroyer-like hull, but was much shorter. In the early part of the Second World War, they were described as Corvettes but they were very good-looking ships, being largely pre-war built, and were of a quality finish. The funnel, with the conspicuous cowl, was typical destroyer design and they were quite correctly used as anti-submarine vessels. With their comparatively high speed of 20 knots, they out-paced the majority of the war-built escorts and frigates. The main armaments of this class were the depth charges, of which up to forty were carried for each depth charge thrower. The design for these sloops is said to have originated from the P-boats of the First World War.

Losses: HMS *Pintail* on 10 June 1914 struck a mine and sank in the Humber Estuary.

HMS *Puffin* on 26 March 1945 rammed and sank a Midget U-boat off the Dutch coast, but was so damaged by the attack that she was written off as a constructive total loss.

Ex-American Coastal Escorts 'Kil' Class

HMS	Ex	USN	Completed	Builder
Kilbirnie	PCE	827	1943	Pullman Standard Car Co. of Chicago
Kilbride	PCE	828	1943	as above
Kilchattan	PCE	829	1943	as above
Kilchrenan	PCE	830	1943	as above
Kildary	PCE	831	1943	as above
Kildwick	PCE	832	1943	as above
Kilham	PCE	833	1943	as above
Kilkenzie	PCE	834	1943	as above
Kilkhampton	PCE	835	1943	as above
Kilmalcolm	PCE	836	1943	as above
Kilmarnock	PCE	837	1943	as above
Kilmartin	PCE	838	1943	as above
Kilmelford	PCE	839	1943	as above
Kilmington	POE	840	1943	as above
Kilmore	POE	841	1943	as above

Specification

Displacement Tons	650
Full load	945
Dimensions	180wl 184½ x 33 x 9½
Armament	Two 3in 50 cal DP/HA in 'A' and 'X' positions
	Two single 40mm bofors
	Two single 20mm
Anti-Submarine	One Hedgehog aft of 'A' gun below the wheelhouse
	Four depth charge throwers
	Two depth charge racks
	Fifty depth charges were carried
Machinery	Diesel engines 1,800bhp to two shafts giving 16 knots
Radius	5,600nm at 10 knots
Fuel	260 tons oil
Complement	104

Class note: These fifteen Coastal Escorts were all that remained of the bulk allocation of 150 ships intended for the Royal Navy, the major share being claimed by the United States Navy. They were built inland at Chicago and, before reaching the sea, had to steam 1,200 miles to the Welland Canal then proceeding to Bermuda for working-up. Some of the class had mechanical troubles but, being new ships straight from the yard, this was not unexpected.

They were to a typical American design with all weapons in bandstands and with the typical pole mast of all US escorts. As an unintentional portent of the future, the hull was not pierced for ports. The hull outline, except for the lack of flare, was similar to the RN escort destroyers of the Hunt Type 4, and was much appreciated in foul weather.

Service note: Vessels of the 'Kil' Class mainly served in the Freetown, Sierra Leone, and Gibraltar sea areas, as reinforcements to escort and anti-submarine groups.

Kilmore.
(National
Maritime
Museum)

Chapter 7

Lake, River and Coastal Gun Boats

Flat Iron Gun Boats 1867–1879

Staunch

Built 1867 Armstrong Mitchell

Specification

Displacement tons	200
Dimensions	75 x 25 x 6½
Armament	One 9in MLR
Machinery	Two two-cylinder engines to two shafts giving 134ihp
Speed	7 knots
Complement	31
Sold	1901

Plucky

Built 1870 HM Dockyard, Portsmouth

Specification

Displacement tons	212
Dimensions	80 x 25 x 6
Armament	One 9in MLR
Machinery	Two two-cylinder engines to two shafts giving 224ihp
Speed	7½ knots
Complement	31
Sold	1928

'Ant' Class

Built 1870–1871

HMS	Builder	Fate
Ant	Laird	Sold 1926
Arrow	Rennie	Sold 1922
Badger	HM Dockyard, Chatham	Sold 1908
Blazer	HM Dockyard, Portsmouth	Sold 1919

Kite. (National Maritime Museum)

Bloodhound	Armstrong	Sold 1921
Bonetta	Rennie	Sold 1909
Bulldog	Campbell Johnston	Sold 1906
Bustard	Napier	Sold 1923
Comet	HM Dockyard, Portsmouth	Sold 1908
Cuckoo	Laird	Sold 1959
Fidget	HM Dockyard, Chatham	Sold 1905
Hyaena	Laird	Sold 1906
Kite	Napier	Sold 1920
Mastiff	Armstrong	Sold 1931
Pickle	Campbell Johnston	Sold 1906
Pike	Campbell Johnston	Sold 1920
Scourge	HM Dockyard, Chatham	Tank vessel C79 1903
Snake	HM Dockyard, Chatham	Cable lighter YC15 1907
Snap	Campbell Johnston	Sold 1909
Weazel	Laird	Oil lighter C118 1904

Specification

Displacement	254 average
Dimensions	85 x 26 x 6½
Armament	One 10in MLR
Machinery	Two cylinder reciprocating engines of 260ihp
Speed	8 knots
Complement	30

'Gadfly' Class

Built 1879

HMS	Builder	Fate
Gadfly	HM Dockyard, Pembroke	Sold 1918
Griper	HM Dockyard, Pembroke	Broken up 1951
Pincher	HM Dockyard, Pembroke	Sold 1905
Tickler	HM Dockyard, Pembroke	Broken up 1937

Specification

Displacement	254 average
Dimensions	85 x 26 x 6½
Armament	One 10in MLR
Machinery	Two cylinder reciprocating engine of 260ihp
Speed	8 knots
Complement	30

'Bouncer' Class

Built 1881

HMS	Builder	Fate
Bouncer	HM Dockyard, Pembroke	Sold 1905
Insolent	HM Dockyard, Pembroke	See 'Loss' below

Specification

Displacement	265
Dimensions	87½ x 26 x 6½
Armament	One 10in MLR
Machinery	Two cylinder reciprocating engine of 260ihp
Speed	8½ knots
Complement	30

Loss: HMS *Insolent* was wrecked on 1 July 1922 in Portsmouth harbour.

'Medina' Class

Built 1876–1877

HMS	Builder	Fate
Dee	Palmer	Sold 1902
Don	Palmer	Sold 1914
Esk	Palmer	Sold 1903
Medina	Palmer	Sold 1904

Medina. (Source not known)

Sabrina	Palmer	Sold 1922
Slaney	Palmer	Sold 1919
Spey	Palmer	Sold 1923
Tay	Palmer	Sold 1920
Tees	Palmer	Sold 1907
Trent	Palmer	Sold 1923
Tweed	Palmer	Sold 1905

Specification

Displacement tons	386
Dimensions	110 x 34 x 5½
Armament	Three 64pdr MLR
Machinery	Two cylinder reciprocating engine of 310ihp
Speed	9½ knots
Complement	51

Note: The term 'Flat Iron', which was given to these gun boats, was because of their alleged similarity in silhouette to a domestic flat iron.

'Heron' Class River Gun Boats

HMS	Launched	Builder
Heron	1897	Yarrow SB
Nightingale	1897	Yarrow SB
Robin	1897	Yarrow SB
Sandpiper	1897	Yarrow SB
Snipe	1897	Yarrow SB

Specification

Displacement tons	85
Dimensions	107¾ x 20 x 2
Armament	Two 6pdr DP, four mg
Machinery	Triple expansion of 240ihp
Speed	9 knots
Fuel	11 tons coal
Complement	25

Note: All built for the China Station and decommissioned in 1914.

Fate: All sold between 1919 and 1928 at Hong Kong.

'Bird' Class River Gun Boats

HMS	Launched	Builder
Moorhen	1901	Yarrow SB
Teal	1901	Yarrow SB
Widgeon	1904	Yarrow SB
Woodcock	1898	Thornycroft
Woodlark	1898	Thornycroft

Specification	*Moorhen, Teal* and *Widgeon*	*Woodcock* and *Woodlark*
Displacement tons	180	150
Dimensions	165 x 24½ x 2¼	148½ x 24 x 2
Armament	Two 6pdr DP, four mg	Two pdr DP, four mg
Machinery	Compound engine of 550ihp	Compound engine of 670ihp
Speed	13 knots	12½ knots
Fuel	36 tons coal	28 tons coal
Complement	37	26

Note: HMS *Woodcock* and HMS *Woodlark* were assembled in England then disassembled and shipped out in pieces and re-launched at Shanghai.

Fate: *Woodcock*, *Woodlark* and *Moorhen* sold between 1928 and 1933 at Hong Kong. *Teal* and *Widgeon* sold 1931 at Shanghai.

Heron. (Yarrow SB)

'P' Class River Gun Boats

HMS	Built	Builder
P50	1916/1917	Beardmore
P51	1916/1917	Beardmore
P52	1916/1917	Caird
P53	1916/1917	Caird
P54	1916/1917	Caird
P55	1916/1917	Caird
P56	1916/1917	Caird
P57	1916/1917	Caird
P58	1916/1917	Not known
P59	1916/1917	Not known
P60	1916/1917	Lobnitz
P61	1916/1917	Lobnitz

Specification

Displacement tons	505
Dimensions	220pp x 30 x 6¼
Armament	One 3pdr (designed two 12pdr)
Machinery	Inclined compound engine of 1,200ihp to a stern paddle wheel
Speed	15 knots
Complement	55

Note: Built for service on the Tigris and Euphrates.
No further information is available on these Gun Boats.

HMS *Guedolen* Gun Boat

HMS	Built	Builder
Guedolen	1897	Not known

Specification

Displacement tons	350
Dimensions	Not known
Armament	Two 6pdr, one 3pdr
Machinery	Not known
Speed	11 knots

Note: Well remembered for the sinking of the German converted lake steamer (to a Gun Boat) SMS *Hermann von Wissman* off Sphinxhaven, Lake Nyasa, on 30 May 1915.

Engagement note: HMS *Guedolen* first attacked the *Hermann von Wissman* on 13 August 1911 and apparently the Germans were not aware that the war had started. The second attack was as mentioned above.

'Fly' Class River Gun Boats

HMS	Shipment of parts	Builder
Blackfly	1916	Yarrow SB
Butterfly	1915	Yarrow SB
Caddisfly	1916	Yarrow SB
Cranefly	1915	Yarrow SB
Dragonfly	1915	Yarrow SB
Firefly	1915	Yarrow SB
Gadfly	1915	Yarrow SB
Grayfly	1915	Yarrow SB
Greenfly	1915	Yarrow SB
Hoverfly	1916	Yarrow SB
Mayfly	1915	Yarrow SB
Sawfly	1915	Yarrow SB
Sedgefly	1916	Yarrow SB
Snakefly	1915	Yarrow SB
Stonefly	1915	Yarrow SB
Waterfly	1915	Yarrow SB

Specification

Displacement tons	98
Dimensions	120pp x 20 x 2
Armament	One 4in DP, one 12pdr DP, one 6pdr DP (not in all), one 3pdr AA, one 2pdr AA, four or five mg

Machinery	Triple expansion engines 175ihp
Speed	9½ knots
Fuel	5 tons coal and 10 tons oil
Complement	22

Note: Due to the shallow draft of the waters in which these Gun Boats were operating, the propeller was in a tunnel. These Gun Boats were built in sections and re-erected at Abadan.

Fate: *Butterfly*, *Cranefly*, *Dragonfly*, *Greenfly*, *Mayfly*, *Sawfly*, *Snakefly*, *Stonefly* and *Sedgefly* all sold 1923 at Basra. *Gadfly* sold to the Air Ministry at Basra in 1922, likewise *Blackfly*, *Greyfly* sold to the War Office 1923. *Waterfly* and *Caddisfly* sold to the Anglo-Persian Oil Co. in 1923 and *Hoverfly* sold to Basra Port Authority in 1923.

Losses: HMS *Firefly* for the period of 1 December 1915 to 26 February 1917 was in Turkish hands but retaken after the latter date by Crown forces. However, on 14 June 1921 was sunk by insurgents in the Euphrates. HM AFV *Blackfly* collided with a bridge at Baghdad and became a constructive total loss while on loan to the Air Ministry.

HMS *Kinsha* (Ex-Commercial)

HMS	Purchased	Builder
Kinsha (ex–*Pioneer*)	1900	Denny

Specification

Displacement tons	616
Dimensions	192½ x 30 x 6¾
Armament	Two 12pdr, seven mg

Kinsha. (National Maritime Museum)

Machinery	Inclined compound engine of 550 driving paddles
Speed	14 knots
Fuel	65 tons coal
Complement	58

Note: Purchased in 1900 for service on the China Station, decommissioned 1914 and sold 1921 at Shanghai.

'Insect' Class River Gun Boats

HMS	Launched	Builder
Aphis	1915	Ailsa SB
Bee	1915	Ailsa SB
Citcala	1915	Barclay Curle
Cockchafer	1915	Barclay Curle
Cricket	1915	Barclay Curle
Glowworm	1916	Barclay Curle
Gnat	1915	Lobnitz
Ladybird	1915	Lobnitz
Mantis	1915	Sunderland SB
Moth	1915	Sunderland SB
Scarab	1915	Wood Skinner
Tarantula	1915	Wood Skinner

Specification

Displacement tons	625
Dimensions	237½ x 36 x 4
Armament	Two 6in on single mountings (in 'A' and 'Y' positions), two 3in AA single superimposed and positioned as 'B' and 'X' guns (see diagram opposite), ten mg
Machinery	Triple expansion 1,000ihp to two shafts giving 14 knots. The propellers were in tunnels due to the shallow draft of these vessels
Fuel	35 tons coal and 54 tons oil. HMS *Moth* – 76 tons oil only
Trial Speed	*Janes* 1931 states '18 knots on trials was easily obtained'
Complement	55

Notes on origin: Also from *Janes*:'These vessels were ordered in February 1915 and built to a design by Yarrow's. Originally intended for service in Salonika, to be dismantled, transported in sections overland and re-erected and re-floated on a tributary of the Danube to fight the Austro–Hungarian Danube Flotilla. To conceal their objective they were ordered as River Gunboats for the Chinese rivers'. Some were towed out to Malta and some made their own way but they were never used for their intended purpose. However, HMS *Glowworm* was mined and suffered damage in 1919 on the

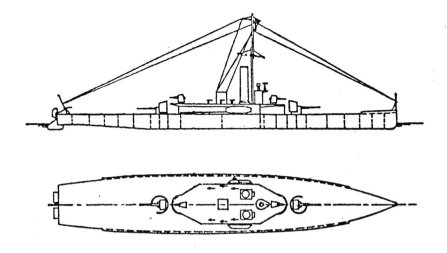

'Insect' Class 1915.

Ladybird. (Imperial War Museum)

Dvina River in North Russia. Others of the class were for a short time in service on the Shatt-el-Arab and the Shatt-el-Bahr (Tigris and Euphrates). They all arrived for some period at the Yangtse Kiang serving on the lower middle, north and west rivers. They were the only Gun Boats with twin funnels, one port and one starboard.

Losses: HMS *Cicala,* while at Hong Kong, was lost after Japanese aircraft attack on 21 December 1941. HMS *Ladybird* was bombed by Italian aircraft, while off Tobruk on 12 May 1941. HMS *Moth* was taken at Hong Kong by the Japanese Navy at the surrender, having been scuttled by own forces on 12 December 1941. She was however raised and salvaged by the Japanese Navy and became HIM *Suma* and was mined off Singapore on 19 March 1945. HMS *Cricket* was mined off Mersa Matruh on 30 June 1941 prior to her conversion for minesweeping. HMS *Cockchafer* was converted for minesweeping at Hong Kong during 1940. Although HMS *Ladybird* was lost to the Royal Navy, she had settled in shallow water and units of our Army used her weapons and her hull as an anti-aircraft platform. HMS *Gnat* became a constructive total loss after being torpedoed by U79 off Bardia, on 21 October 1941 but she was not scrapped until 1945.

Yangtse note: After the commencement or the undeclared war between China and Japan from 1932 and later, all our River Gun Boats were adapted for minesweeping against mines sown by the Chinese Navy to protect the booms which they built across the river.

Minelaying: HMS *Aphis* was employed as a minelayer in the Mediterranean on at least one occasion off Bomba in the Second World War.

Gun protection: The 3in and 6in guns were mounted in shields and the mg had bullet-proof plating guards retrofitted as required. Sniper-proof plating was also fitted as and when occasion demanded on all RN River Gun Boats.

'Seamew' Class River Gun Boats

HMS	Launched	Builder
Seamew	1928	Yarrow
Tern	1927	Yarrow
Gannet	1927	Yarrow
Peterel	1927	Yarrow

Specification	*Seamew* and *Tern*	*Gannet* and *Peterel*
Displacement	287	345
Dimensions	160wl x 167½ x 27 x 3¼	177wl x 184¾ x 29 x 3¼
Armament	Two 3in AA on single mtgs and eight mg on all four ships	
Machinery	Two shaft geared turbines 1,370shp	Two shaft geared turbines 2,120shp
Speed	14 knots	16 knots
Fuel	50 tons oil	60 tons oil
Complement	55	60

Naming note: HMS *Peterel* was named so due to an error in the shipyard, but should have been named *Petrel*.

Losses: HM *Peterel* on 8 December 1941 was the sole remaining Royal Navy vessel at Shanghai and news of the Japanese attack on Pearl Harbor was not received aboard until two hours after the event. The Chief of Staff to the C-in-C on HIM *Idzumo* requested the surrender of *Peterel* but was refused this by her commanding officer. Minutes later the Japanese heavy cruiser had opened fire and *Peterel* was soon blazing fiercely from stem to stern. HMS *Peterel* slowly keeled over and sank beneath the flames

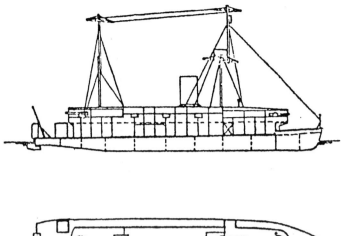

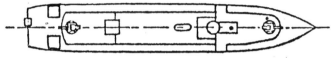

'Seamew' Class 1927.

Tern. (Yarrow SB)

of the burning oil from her fuel tanks. The Japanese also directed small arms fire at the survivors in the water. HMS *Tern* on 19 December 1941 was scuttled by own forces at Hong Kong in the face of the Japanese advance.

HMS *Falcon* **River Gun Boat**

HMS	Launched	Builder
Falcon	1931	Yarrow

Specification

Displacement tons	354
Dimensions	146pp 150 x 28¾ x 4¾
Armament.	One 3.7in howitzer, two 6pdr on single mountings, ten mg
Machinery	Two shaft geared turbines 2,250shp giving 15 knots
Fuel	84 tons oil
Complement	58

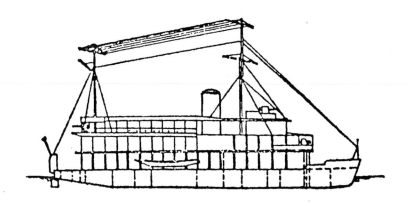

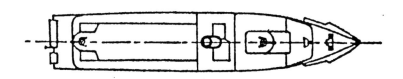

'Falcon' Class 1931.

Falcon. (Yarrow SB)

'Sandpiper' Class River Gun Boats

HMS	Launched	Builder
Sandpiper	1933	Thornycroft
Robin	1934	Yarrow

Specification	Robin	Sandpiper
Displacement tons	226	185
Dimensions	150pp x 26¾ x 3	160pp x 30¾ x 1¾
Armament	One 3.7in Howitzer, one 6pdr single mounting, eight mg both ships	
Machinery	Two shaft VTE reciprocating (both ships)	
	800ihp	650ihp
Speed	12¾ knots	11¼ knots
Complement	35	32

Loss: HMS *Robin* was scuttled by own forces at Hong Kong on 25 December 1941 in the face of the Japanese advance.

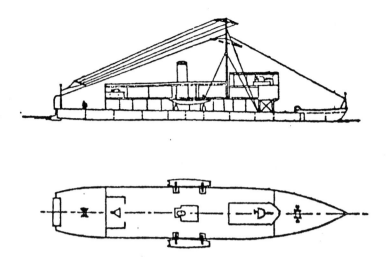

'Sandpiper' Class 1933.

Robin. (Yarrow SB)

'Dragonfly' Class River Gun Boats

HMS	Launched	Builder
Dragonfly	1938	Thornycroft
Grasshopper	1939	Thornycroft
Locust	1939	Yarrow
Mosquito	1939	Yarrow
Scorpion	1937	White

Building of *Bee* of this class at the yard of J.S. White was cancelled in March 1940.

Specification		*Scorpion*
Displacement tons	585	670
Dimensions	197 x 33 x 5	208¾ x 34½ x 5
Armament	Two 4in on single mountings, one 3.7in Howitzer, eight mg	Two 4in on single mountings, two 3pdr on single mountings, one 3.7in Howitzer
Machinery	Two shaft geared turbines 3,800shp	Two shaft geared turbines 4,500shp
Speed	17 knots	17 knots
Complement	74	93

Losses: HMS *Mosquito* on 1 June 1940 was bombed by German aircraft off Dunkirk. HMS *Dragonfly* and HMS *Grasshopper* were bombed and sunk by Japanese aircraft on the 14 February 1942, south of Singapore. HMS *Scorpion* was sunk in a surface action with a Japanese destroyer in the Banka Straits on 13 February 1942.

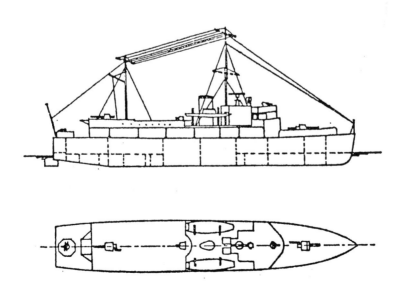

'Dragonfly' Class 1938.

Dragonfly. (Vosper Thornycroft)

Locust. (Yarrow S.B.)

Scorpion. (J. Samuel White)

Ex-Persian River Gun Boats

RINS	Ex-Persian	Completed	Builder
Hira	*Chahbazz*	1931	Cant Nay Ruiniti
Lal	*Simorgh*	1931	Cant Partenopei
Moti	*Karkas*	1931	Cant Partenopei
Nilam	*Charokh*	1931	Cant Partenopei

Specification

Displacement tons	331
Dimensions	170pp x 22 x 5¾ mean
Armament (Designed)	Two 76mm and two pom poms AA
Armament	One 12pdr (3in) DP, one 20mm AA
Machinery	Two Fiat diesels each to one shaft of 450bhp
Speed	15½ knots
Range	3,000nm at 8 knots
Complement	45 approx

Naming: *Janes* of 1931 gives the Persian names (in sequence) as *Raker, Simorgh, Karkas* and *Charokh*.

Note: During operations of Crown forces in Persia (now Iran) in the Second World War, the above Gun Boats were captured by the Royal Navy and commissioned into the RIM as RINS ships.

Construction: Understood only built for river and estuarial operations and unsuitable for the open sea.

Simorgh. (Fototeca)

Nilam. (Fototeca)

Chapter 8

Motor Anti-Submarine Boats

Motor Anti-Submarine Boats, British Power Boat Co.

Motor Anti-Submarine Boats 1, 2, 3, 4 and 5

Built 1938–1939

Specification

Dimensions	60¼ x 13¼ x 2¾
Armament	Two .303in mg
Anti-submarine	Depth charges
Machinery	Two shaft petrol engines 1,000bhp
Speed	25 knots
Complement	9

Note: In the early days of the Second World War, MA/SBs played an important part in the hunt for U-boats but, as the war progressed and groups of frigates and sloops became available for hunting U-boats, so the need for the MA/SB declined, and by 1943 the type was virtually extinct.

Anti-submarine weapons: The most efficient A/S weapon carried was the standard depth charge. Numbers varied from craft to craft but were launched from the beam and the stern.

Loss: HM MA/SB3 was mined on 28 February 1941 in the Suez Canal and had to be beached as a constructive total loss.

Motor Anti-Submarine Boats 6, 7, 8, 9, 10, 11, 12, 13, 14, 15, 16, 17, 18, 19, 20 and 21

Built 1939–1940

Specification

Displacement tons	23
Dimensions	70 x 20 x 4
Armament	Eight .303in mg
Anti-submarine	As MA/SB1
Machinery	Two shaft petrol engines, 1,000bhp
Speed	23 knots
Complement	9

Note: These were all converted to MGBs in late 1940.

MA/SB1. (P.A. Vicary)

MA/SB5. (R. Perkins)

Motor Anti-Submarine Boats 22, 23, 24, 25, 26, 27, 28, 29, 30, 31, 32, 33, 34, 35, 36, 37, 38, 39 and 49

Built 1941

Specification

Displacement tons	20
Dimensions	63 x 15 x 4¼
Armament	Two .303in mg
Anti-submarine	As MA/SB1
Machinery	Two shaft petrol engines, 1,000bhp
Speed	25 knots
Complement	9

Loss: HM MA/SB30 struck the Humber boom on 14 December 1941 and later foundered.

Motor Anti-Submarine Boats, J.S. White & Co.

Motor Anti-Submarine Boats 47 and 48

Built 1940

Specification

Displacement tons	39
Dimensions	75 x 16½ x 4½
Armament	Eight .303in mg
Anti-submarine	Depth charges
Machinery	Three shaft petrol engines, 3,450bhp
Speed	42/38 knots
Complement	9

Note: These two MA/SBs were being built in England for the Polish Navy, but were taken over by the Admiralty and converted to MTBs.

Motor Anti-Submarine Boats 40, 41, 42 and 43 were building in England for the Royal Norwegian Navy as nos 1, 2, 3 and 4. Nos 44 and 45 were building for the Royal Swedish Navy as T1 and T2. However, all six craft were taken over by the Admiralty and converted to MGBs.

Motor Anti-Submarine Boat 46 was under construction in England for the Royal Netherlands Navy but was taken over by the Admiralty and completed as an MGB.

Motor Anti-Submarine Boats 50, 51, 52, 53, 54, 55, 56, 57, 58, 59, 60, 61, 62, 63, 64, 65, 66 and 67 were all building in England for the French Navy but were taken over by the Admiralty and completed as MGBs.

MA/SBs 64 and 60. (Imperial War Museum)

Motor Anti-Submarine Boats 74, 75, 76, 77, 78, 79, 80, 81, 82, 83, 84, 85, 86, 87, 88, 89, 90, 91, 92 and 97 were all cancelled after being ordered in 1941. Nos 74 to 93 were later allocated to new MGBs, and nos 94 to 97 were not used.

Ex-French Submarine Chasers

HMS	Ex-French	Completed	Builder
CH5 (later *Carentan*)	CH5	1939/1940	Fge. & Ch. de la Mediterranee
CH6	CH6	1939/1940	Fge. & Ch. de la Mediterranee
CH7	CH7	1939/1940	Fge. & Ch. de la Mediterranee
CH8 (later *Rennes*)	CH8	1939/1940	Fge. & Ch. de la Mediterranee
CH9	CH9	1939/1940	At. & Ch. de France
CH10 (later *Bayonne*)	CH10	1939/1940	At. & Ch. de France
CH11 (later *Boulogne*)	CH11	1939/1940	At. & Ch. de France
CH12 (later *Benodet*)	CH12	1939/1940	At. & Ch. de France
CH13 (later *Calais*)	CH13	1939/1940	Ch. Worms
CH14 (later *Dielette*)	CH14	1939/1940	Ch. Worms
CH15 (later *Paimpol*)	CH15	1939/1940	Ch. Worms
CH16	CH16	1939/1940	Ch. Worms

Specification

Displacement tons	107
Dimensions	121¾ x 17½ x 6½

Armament	One 75mm, one 2pdr, two 20mm, four .303in mg
Anti–submarine	Depth charges were carried
Machinery	Two shaft diesel engines, 1,130bhp
Speed	16 knots
Complement	28

Note: These Submarine Chasers arrived in England at the fall of France with their French crews and were commissioned into the Royal Navy. After a time eight of these vessels were manned by the Free French and the remainder by RN and Polish crews.

Construction note: All constructed of steel.

Losses: FFS *Carentan* foundered in heavy weather on 21 December 1943 off the Dorset coast.

CH6 and CH7, while under the Polish flag, were lost in the English Channel during October 1940.

FFS Rennes was bombed in the English Channel on 13 July 1942. HMS CH9 was bombed off Dunkirk on 21 May 1940.

RFS CR 16 was scuttled in Croix Roads on 18 June 1940.

HMS	Ex–French	Completed	Builder
CH41 (later *Audierne*)	CH41	1940	Ch. Normandie (Fecamp)
CH42 (later *Larmor*)	CH42	1940	Ch. Normandie (Fecamp)
CH43 (later *Levandou*)	CH43	1940	Ch. Normandie (Fecamp)

Specification

Displacement tons	126
Dimensions	122¾ x 17½ x 8
Armament	One 75mm, one 2pdr, two 20mm, four .303in mg
Machinery	Two shaft diesel engines, 1,130bhp
Speed	16 knots
Complement	29

Note: All constructed of wood (see note for the CH5 Class above).

Chapter 9

Motor Gun Boats

Motor Gun Boats, British Power Boat Co.

Motor Gun Boats 6, 7, 8, 9, 10, 11, 12, 13, 14, 15, 16, 17, 18, 19, 20 and 21

Built 1940 ex-MA/SBs

Specification

Displacement tons	31
Dimensions	70 x 20 x 4
Armament	One 2pdr or one 20mm or four .303in mg and four .5in mg
Machinery	Two shaft petrol engines 1,900bhp
Speed	23 knots
Complement	10

Losses: HM MGB12 was mined off Milford Haven on 3 February 1941.

HM MGB17 was mined off Normandy on 11 June 1944.

HM MGB18 sank after a surface action off Terschelling on 30 September 1942.

HM MGB9 while slipped for repairs in an Allied port on 6 November 1942 was bombed by enemy aircraft.

Motor Gun Boats 74, 75, 76, 77, 78, 79, 80 and 81

Built 1942

Specification

Displacement tons	47
Dimensions	71¾ x 20¾ x 5
Armament	One 2pdr, two 20mm, four .303in mg
Machinery	Three shaft petrol engines, 4,050/3,600bhp
Speed	40/35 knots
Complement	12

Note: These were the first Motor Gun Boats to be designed as such.

Losses: HM MGB76 sank after surface action on 6 October 1942 in the North Sea.

HM MGB78 was damaged during a surface action with enemy forces on 3 October 1942 and had to be beached on the Dutch coast.

HM MGB79 sank after surface action off the Hook of Holland on 28 February 1943.

MGB14.
(World Ship
Society)

MGB16.
(Wright &
Logan)

MGB75.
(Imperial
War
Museum)

Motor Gun Boats 107, 108, 109, 110, 111, 112, 113, 114, 115, 116, 117, 118, 119, 120, 121, 122, 123, 124, 125, 126, 127, 128, 129, 130, 131, 132, 133, 134, 135, 136, 137, 138, 139, 140, 141, 142, 143, 144, 145, 146, 147, 148, 149, 150, 151, 152, 153, 154, 155, 156, 157, 158, 159, 160, 161, 162, 163, 164, 165, 166, 167, 168, 169, 170, 171, 172, 173, 174, 175 and 176

Built 1942

Specification

Displacement tons	37
Dimensions	71¾ x 20½ x 3/5¾
Armament	One 2pdr, two 20mm, four .303in mg but some of these boats were fitted while under construction with two 18in torpedo tubes
Machinery	Three shaft petrol engines, 4,050bhp
Speed	42/36½ knots
Complement	12

Losses: HM MGB109 was mined off Dover and became a constructive total loss on 7 February 1943.

HM MGB110 was in action with German surface craft off Dunkirk on 29 May 1943.

MGB116. (World Ship Society)

MGB123. (World Ship Society)

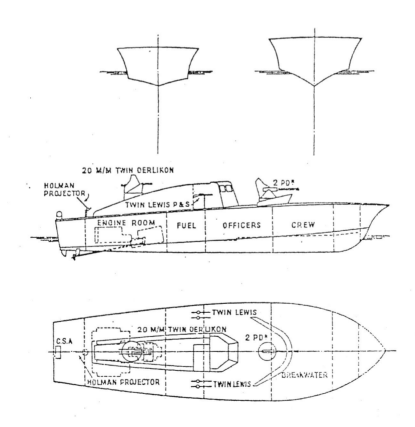

Outline of 71ft 6in MGB.

Motor Gun Boats, Camper & Nicholson Ltd

Motor Gun Boats 511, 512, 513, 514, 515, 516, 517 and 518

Built 1944

Specification

Displacement tons	115
Dimensions	117 x 22½ x 3¾/4½
Armament	Two 6pdr, four 20mm
Torpedo tubes	four 18in
Machinery	Three shaft petrol engines, 4,050bhp
Speed	31/26 knots
Complement	30

Ex-American Motor Gun Boats

Motor Gun Boat 68

Built 1940

Specification

Displacement tons	34
Dimensions	81 x 20 x 5½
Armament	One 20mm, six .5in mg
Machinery	Three shaft petrol engines, 3,750bhp
Speed	40/35 knots
Complement	14

Note: Built in the United States as PT6 (II).
Built by Higgins (New Orleans).

Motor Gun Boats 82, 83, 84, 85, 86, 87, 88, 89, 90, 91, 92 and 93

Built 1941

Specification

Displacement tons	45
Dimensions	77 x 20 x 5½
Armament	One 20mm, four .5in mg, four .303 mg
Machinery	Three shaft petrol engines, 4,050bhp
Speed	40/35 knots
Complement	12

Note: All transferred to the Royal Navy under Lease Lend and were in sequence PTC1–12.

MGB86. (Wright & Logan)

Losses: HM MGB 90, caught fire at Portland on 16 July 1941
All built by Higgins (New Orleans) but designed by the Electric Boat Co.

Motor Gun Boats 177, 178, 179, 180, 181, 182, 183, 184, 185, 186, 187, 188, 189, 190 and 191

Built in 1942

Specification

Displacement tons	46
Dimensions	81¼ x 20 x 5¾
Armament	Two 20mm, four .5in mg, four .303in mg
Machinery	Three shaft petrol engines, 4,050bhp
Speed	42/36 knots
Complement	12

Note: All transferred to the Royal Navy under the Lease Lend programme and in sequence were PT206, 214, 215, 216, 201, 204, 207, 208, 209, 211, 213, 217, 203, 205, 210 and 212.

Built by Higgins (New Orleans).

Motor Gun Boats 69, 70, 71, 72 and 73

Built 1940

Specification

Displacement tons	30
Dimensions	69½ x 19 x 4½
Armament	One 20mm, four .5in mg
Machinery	Three shaft petrol engines, 1,500bhp
Speed	27 knots
Complement	12

Note: These boats were under construction in the United States for the Finnish Navy but, after the alliance of Finland with Germany, were not delivered. They were transferred to the Royal Navy under the Lease Lend agreement.

Their Finnish numbers would have been RB1-5.

Built by Higgins (New Orleans).

Motor Gun Boats 100, 101, 102, 103, 104, 105 and 106

Built 1941

Specifications

Displacement tons	30
Dimensions	69½ x 19 x 4½
Armament	One 20mm, four .5in mg
Machinery	Three shaft petrol engines, 1,500bhp
Speed	27 knots
Complement	12

Note: These boats were building in the United States for the Finnish Navy as RB6–12 and were transferred to the Royal Navy under Lease Lend in 1941.

Built by Higgins (New Orleans).

Ex-French Motor Gun Boats

Motor Gun Boats 98 and 99 were converted French MTBs which had been towed to the UK around the period of the capitulation of France in 1940.

HM MGB	Converted	Builder
98 (ex-VTB11)	1940	Chantiers; Ateliers Loire
99 (ex-VTB12)	1940	Chantiers; Ateliers Loire

Specification (as built)

Displacement tons	28
Dimensions	65ft (length)
Armament	Two 7.5mm mg
Torpedo tubes	Two 400mm
Anti-submarine	Six 35kg depth charges
Machinery	Two shaft Lorraine petrol engines 2,200bhp
Speed	45 knots
Complement	14 approx

Losses: HM MGB98 was bombed by enemy aircraft at Portsmouth in March 1941.
HM MGB99 was lost in April 1945, place and cause not known.

Motor Gun Boats 50, 51, 52, 53, 54, 55, 56, 57, 58, 59, 60, 61, 62, 63, 64, 65, 66 and 67

Built 1940–1941

Specification

Displacement tons	28
Dimensions	70 x 20 x 4
Armament	One 20mm or four .303in mg four .5in mg, four .303in mg
Machinery	Three shaft petrol engines 3,300bhp
Speed	40/36 knots
Complement	12

Note: All under construction in England for the French Navy as Motor Anti-Submarine Boats but taken over by the Admiralty and completed as MGBs.

Losses: HM MGB62 was in collision with MGB67 on 9 August 1941 in the North Sea.
HM MGB64 foundered in heavy weather off Ostend, on 8 August 1943.

Built by British Power Boat Co. (Hythe).

MGB51.
(Imperial
War
Museum)

Ex-Netherlands Motor Gun Boats

Motor Gun Boat 46

Built 1940

Specification

Displacement tons	35
Dimensions	70 x 20 x 4¼
Armament	One 2pdr, four .5in mg
Machinery	Three shaft petrol engines 3,300/3,000bhp
Speed	42/39 knots
Complement	9

Note: This boat was under construction in England for the Royal Netherlands Navy as a
Motor Anti-Submarine Boat but was taken over by the Admiralty.
Built by British Power Boat Co. (Hythe).

Ex-Norwegian Motor Gun Boats

Motor Gun Boats 40, 41, 42 and 43

Built 1940

Specification

Displacement tons	24
Dimensions	63 x 15 x 4¼
Armament	One 2pdr 4.5in mg
Machinery	Two shaft petrol engines, 2,200bhp
Speed	40/36 knots
Complement	10

MGB43.
(Wright &
Logan)

Note: All built in England for the Royal Norwegian Navy as Motor Anti-Submarine
   Boats but taken over by the Royal Navy.
Built by British Power Boat Co. (Hythe).

Ex-Polish Gun Boats

Motor Gun Boats 47 and 48

Built 1940

Specification

Displacement tons	39
Dimensions	70 x 16½ x 4½
Armament	One 20 mm, four .5in mg, four .303in mg
Machinery	Three shaft petrol engines, 3,450bhp
Speed	42/38 knots
Complement	12

Note: Both were under construction in England for the Polish Navy as Motor Anti-
   Submarine Boats but were taken over by the Admiralty.
Built by J.S. White (Cowes).

Ex-Swedish Motor Gun Boats

Motor Gun Boats 44 and 45

Built 1940

Specification

Displacement tons	24
Dimensions	63 x 15 x 4½
Armament	One 4pdr four .5in mg
Machinery	One shaft petrol engine 2,200bhp
Speed	40/36 knots
Complement	10

Note: Both were under construction in England for the Royal Swedish Navy as Motor
   Anti-Submarine Boats but were taken over by the Admiralty.
Built by British Power Boat Co. (Hythe).

Ex-Turkish Motor Gun Boats

Motor Gun Boats 502, 503 and 509

Built 1942

Boats 504–508 were completed as Mercantile Blockade Runners, and were named in sequence: MVs *Hopewell, Nonsuch, Gay Viking, Gay Corsair* and *Master Standfast* and flew the Red Ensign.

Specification

Displacement tons	95
Dimensions	117 x 20¼ x 3¾ / 4¾
Armament	Boats 502, 503 and 509: One 2pdr, four .5in mg, four .303in mg
Torpedo tubes	Two 21in
Machinery	Three shaft diesel engines, 3,000bhp
Speed	30/27 knots but MGB509 with three shaft petrol engines 4,050bhp gave 30 knots
Complement	(all craft) 21
Armament (Named Boats)	Two 20mm, four .303in mg, and could carry 45 tons of cargo
Speed	27 knots

Note: These boats were building in England for the Turkish Navy but were taken over by the Admiralty. The named boats were used for blockade running from the UK to Sweden.

Losses: MV *Gay Viking* on 5 February 1945 when off Kristiansand was in collision with MV *Hopewell*, the latter becoming a constructive total loss.

MV *Master Standfast* was captured by the German Patrol Boat V1606 off Lysekil on 5 November 1943.

Blockade Runner. (Imperial War Museum)

MGB502. (Imperial War Museum)

HM MGB502 (as MGB2002) was mined on 12 May 1945 in the Skagerak.

HM MGB507 (as MGB2007) became stranded off Aberdeen on 22 May 1945 and broke up.

Built by Camper & Nicholson (Northam).

Motor Gun Boats, Experimental Boats

Motor Gun Boat 501

Built 1943

Specification

Displacement tons	95
Dimensions	117 x 19½ x 3¼/4½
Armament (Designed)	One 3in, one 2pdr, two 21in torpedo tubes
Armament (Actual)	One 2pdr, one 20mm, four .5in mg
Torpedo tubes	Two 21in
Machinery	Three shaft petrol engines 3,750bhp
Speed	32/29 knots
Complement	21

Note: Was designed as a combined Motor Anti-Submarine Boat and Motor Torpedo Boat but completed as an MGB.

Loss: HM MGB501 sank after an internal explosion on 27 July 1942 when off Lands End.

Built by Camper & Nicholson (Gosport).

Motor Gun Boat 510

Built 1943

Specification

Displacement tons	75
Dimensions	100½ x 19 x 5½
Armament	One 6pdr, two 20 mm, four .303in mg
Torpedo tubes	Two 18in
Machinery	Four shaft petrol engines, 5,000bhp
Speed	35 knots
Complement	20

Note: Was a one-boat class for heavy armament and higher speed which necessitated four shafts to the normal three.

Built by Vosper (Portsmouth).

Admiralty Type (RE) Built

HMS	Completed	Builder
Pamela	1945	Royal Engineers
Una	1945	Royal Engineers

Specification

Displacement tons	40
Dimensions	52 x 13 x 2¼
Armament	One 40mm, one 20mm and four .303in mg on two twin mountings
Machinery	Three shaft petrol engines 195bhp
Speed	10 knots

MGB510.
(Vosper
Thornycroft)

Note: Two of four planned for construction by the Royal Engineers on the Chindwin
River in Burma for the Royal Navy.

Cancellations: The third craft was broken up unfinished and the fourth was not
commenced.

Role: May be described as Support Motor Gun Boats (SMGB).

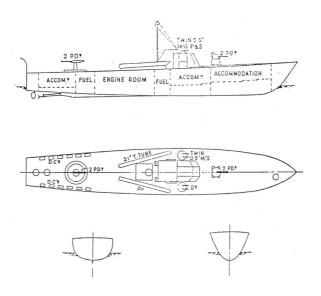

Outline of MGB501.

Pamela and *Una*. (MOD)

Chapter 10

Steam Gun Boats

Steam Gun Boats (SGBs)

HMS	Launched	Builder
SGB3 (later *Grey Seal*)	1941	Yarrow
SGB4 (later *Grey Fox*)	1941	Yarrow
SGB5 (later *Grey Owl*)	1941	Hawthorn Leslie
SGB6 (later *Grey Shark*)	1941	Hawthorn Leslie
SGB7	1941	Denny
SGB8 (later *Grey Wolf*)	1941	Denny
SGB9 (later *Grey Goose*)	1942	White

Grey Owl. (Swan Hunter)

Grey Shark. (Swan Hunter)

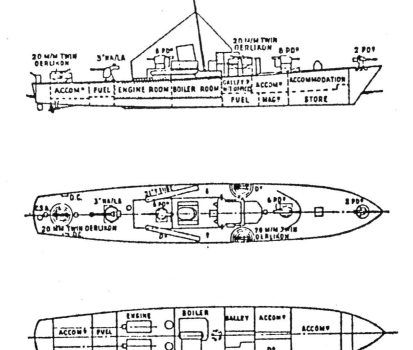

Outline of Steam Gun Boat.

Specification

Displacement Tons	165
Dimensions	145½ x 20 x 5½
Armament (Designed)	Two 2pdr on single mountings, four .5in mg on two twin mountings
Torpedo tubes	Two 21in torpedo tubes, one either beam of the wheelhouse, to discharge forward
Machinery	Geared turbines, 8,000, excepting boats 7, 8 and 9 with 7,220, all shp, to two shafts, giving 35 knots
Complement	27

Loss: HM SGB7, while on night patrol in the English Channel, came into action with enemy light forces on 19 June 1942 and, after an exchange of fire, was lost.

Chapter 11

Motor Torpedo Boats

Motor Torpedo Boats, British Power Boat Co.

Motor Torpedo Boats 1, 2, 3, 4, 5, 6, 7, 8, 9, 10, 11, 12, 14, 15, 16, 17, 18 and 19

Built 1936–1939

Specification

Displacement tons	22
Dimensions	60¼ x 13¼ x 2¾
Armament	Eight .303in mg in two quad dustbins
Torpedo tubes	Two 18in
Machinery	Three shaft petrol motors, 1,800/1,500bhp
Speed	33/29 knots
Complement	9

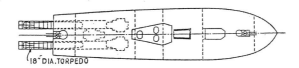

Outline of 60ft MTB.

MTB01.
(Wright &
Logan)

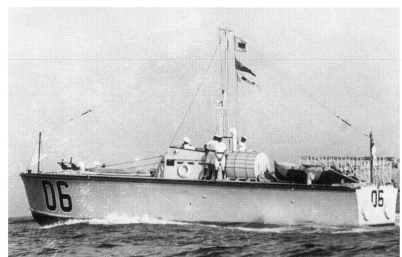

MTB06.
(Source not
known)

Note: Engine output and speed. On the majority of MTBs and MGBs the engines were
limited to an absolute maximum rating for a very short time, in some cases as little as
fifteen minutes, this being indicated by the larger bhp quoted and the higher speed.
For normal continuous maximum speed, which could be kept up for hours, the lesser
bhp was delivered, thus giving the lesser maximum speed.

Losses: HM MTB6 foundered in heavy weather off Sardinia on 16 November 1939.

HM MTB7 was scuttled in the face of the Japanese advance at Hong Kong on
26 December 1941.

HM MTB8 was destroyed by own forces at Hong Kong in the face of the
Japanese advance on the 16 December 1941.

HM MTBs 9, 10 and 11 all as MTB7.

HM MTB12 sank after surface action with Japanese landing craft off Hong Kong on 19 December 1941.

HM MTB15 was mined in the Thames Estuary on 24 September 1940.

HM MTB16 as MTB15 on 31 October 1940.

HM MTB17 was mined off Ostend on 21 October 1940.

Built by British Power Boat Co. (Hythe).

Motor Torpedo Boats 412, 413, 414, 415, 416, 417 and 418

Built 1942

Specification

Displacement tons	46
Dimensions	71¾ x 23¾ x 5
Armament	One 2pdr, two 20mm, four .303in mg
Torpedo tubes	Two 18in
Machinery	Three shaft petrol engines, 3,600bhp
Speed	39 knots
Complement	17

Note: Guns were mounted singly or twin as in MTB1. Four .303in mg in a small turret similar to an aircraft gun turret. These were known as 'dustbins'.

Losses: HM MTB412 was lost by collision when in action on 27 July 1944 off the Normandy beachhead.

HM MTB417 sank after a surface action with E-boats or similar off Calais on 16 March 1944.

All built by British Power Boat Co. (Hythe).

MTBs 416 and 413. (Imperial War Museum)

Motor Torpedo Boats 430, 431, 432, 434, 435, 436, 437, 438, 439, 440, 441, 442, 443, 444, 445, 446, 447, 448, 449, 450, 451, 452, 453, 454, 455, 456, 457, 458, 459, 460, 461, 462, 463, 464, 465, 466, 467, 468, 469, 470, 471, 472, 473, 474, 475, 476, 477, 478, 479, 481, 481, 482, 483, 484, 485, 486, 487, 488, 489, 490, 491, 492, 493, 494, 495, 496, 497, 498, 499, 500, 502, 503, 504, 505, 506, 507, 508, 509, 519, 520, 521 and 522

Built 1942–1945

Specification

Displacement tons	37 to No.457, 41 to No.492, and 44 thereafter
Dimensions	71¾ x 20½ x 5¾
Armament	One 2pdr, two 20mm, four .303in mg to No.457. One 6pdr, two 20mm, four .303in mg thereafter
Torpedo tubes	Two 18in
Machinery	Three shaft petrol engines, 3,600bhp
Speed	39 knots
Complement	17

Losses: HM MTB430 was rammed by an E-boat off the Normandy beachhead on 27 July 1944.

HM MTB434 sank after a surface action with E-boats or similar off Normandy on 9 July 1944.

HM MTB448 was bombed in error by Allied aircraft off Normandy. on 11 June 1944

HM MTBs 438 and 444 were lost after a fire at Ostend on 14 February 1945.

HM MTBs 459, 460, 461 and 462 (all manned by the RCN) as 438 and 434.

HM MTB463 (when manned by the RCN) was mined on 8 July 1944 off Normandy.

HM MTB465 as 438 (manned by RCN).

HM MTB494 on 7 April 1945 was rammed by an E-boat in the North Sea.

HM MTB493 became a constructive total loss on 7 April 1945 after ramming an E-boat in the North Sea.

Built by British Power Boat Co. (Hythe).

Camper & Nicholson Ltd Motor Torpedo Boats

Motor Torpedo Boats 511, 512, 513, 514, 515, 516, 517 and 518

Built 1944

Specification

Displacement tons	115
Dimensions	117 x 22¼ x 3¾/4½
Armament	Two 6pdr, four 20mm
Torpedo tubes	Four 18in

MTB521. (Wright & Logan)

MTB522. (Source not known)

Machinery	Three shaft petrol engines, 4,050bhp
Speed	31/26 knots
Complement	30

Note: Built as interchangeable MTB/MGBs.
Built by Camper & Nicholson (Gosport).

MTB513. (Foto Flite)

MTB516. (Foto Flite)

J.I. Thornycroft & Co. Motor Torpedo Boats

Motor Torpedo Boats 24, 25 and 28

Built 1939–1940 (No.23 of this class was sold and No.28 was its replacement)

Specification

Displacement tons	37
Dimensions	72 x 16½ x 3¾
Armament	Four .5 mg
Torpedo tubes	Two 21in
Machinery	Three shaft petrol engines, 3,600/3,450bhp
Speed	42/40 knots
Complement	10

Loss: HM MTB28 was lost by fire on 7 March 1941 at Portsmouth.
Built by Thornycroft (Hampton).

Motor Torpedo Boats 49, 50, 51, 52, 53, 54, 55 and 56

Built 1941

Specification

Displacement tons	52
Dimensions	75½ x 16½ x 2¼/5½

MTB28. (National Maritime Museum)

Armament	Two .5in mg, two .303in mg
Torpedo tubes	Two 21in
Machinery	Two shaft with two petrol engines to each shaft, 2,600bhp
Speed	29 knots
Complement	12

Note: These craft were all converted into Target Towing Launches for the War Office. Built by Thornycroft (Hampton).

Motor Torpedo Boats 213, 214, 215, 216 and 217

Built 1940/1941

Specification

Displacement tons	17
Dimensions	55 x 11 x 3¼
Armament	Four .303in mg
Torpedoes	Two 18in in troughs
Machinery	Two shaft petrol engines, 1,200bhp
Speed	40 knots
Complement	5

Losses: HM MTB213 and 214 sank after German aircraft attack on 23 May 1941 at Suda Bay.
HM MTB215 lost (date, place and cause unknown) in the Mediterranean and paid off 29 March 1942.
HM MTBs 216 and 217 as 213.
Built by Thornycroft (Hampton).

Vosper Ltd Motor Motor Torpedo Boats

Motor Torpedo Boats 20, 21, 22, 23, 29 and 30

Built 1939–1940

Specification

Displacement tons	35¾
Dimensions	70 x 14¾ x 3¾/5
Armament	Four .5in mg
Torpedo tubes	Two 21in
Machinery	Three shaft petrol engines, 3,600/3,450bhp
Speed	42/40 knots
Complement	10

MTB23. (Vosper Thornycroft)

MTB30. (Vosper Thornycroft)

Note: Boats 20, 21 and 23 were sold to the Royal Romanian Navy in 1940 and boats 29
    and 30 were built as replacements for 20 and 21.

Losses: HM MTB29 on 6 October 1942 was in collision with an E-boat in the North
        Sea.

        HM MTB30 on 18 December 1942 was mined in the North Sea.

MTBs 20–23 were built by Vosper (Portsmouth) and 29 and 30 were built by Camper &
    Nicholson (Gosport).

Motor Torpedo Boats 31, 32, 33, 34, 35, 36, 37, 38, 39, 40, 57, 58, 59, 60, 61, 62, 63, 64, 65 and 66

Built 1940–1942

Specification

Displacement tons	39
Dimensions	70 x 14¾ x 3¼/5
Armament	Two .5in mg, four .303in mg, but boats 57–66 had one 20mm in lieu of a .303in 'dustbin', with two .5in added midships and two .303in added forward
Torpedo tubes	Two 21in, but No.61 had her torpedo tubes removed and three 20mm added in lieu upon her conversion to an MGB
Machinery	Three shaft petrol engines, 3,600/3,450bhp for boats 31, 32, 33 and 34. Boats 35 and later had Hall Scott petrol engines, 1,800bhp
Speed	40/38 knots, boats 31, 32, 33 and 34. Boat 35 and later 25 knots
Complement	12

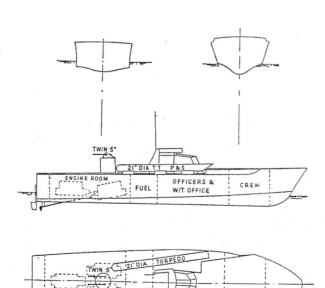

MTB31. (Vosper Thornycroft)

MTB38. (World Ship Society)

Opposite: Outline of early 70ft MTB.

Note: The difference in engine power of the earlier four boats compared with the later was due to Italy entering the war – the Isotta Fraschini petrol engines which were used in many of the Coastal Forces craft were no longer obtainable.

Losses: HM MTBs 33, 37, 39 and 40 were all bombed by German aircraft when completing at Portsmouth in 1941.

HM MTB61 was wrecked off Kelibia on 9 May 1943.

HM MTBs 63 and 64 were lost on 2 April 1943 after collision when off Benghazi.

Motor Torpedo Boats 218, 219, 220 and 221

Built 1940–1941

Specification

Displacement tons	35
Dimensions	70 x 14¾ x 3¼/5
Armament	Ten .303in mg, two 'dustbins' and two singles
Torpedo tubes	Two 21in
Machinery	Two shaft petrol engines, 2,300bhp
Speed	27½ knots
Complement	10

Note: Originally designed for three shafts/engines but, due to the shortage of Italian IF engines, they were downgraded (see Ex-Greek MTBs for origin).

Losses: HM MTB218 was mired in the Straits of Dover on 18 August 1942.

HM MTB220 sank after a surface action with E Boats or similar off Ambleteuse.

Built by Vosper (Portsmouth).

MTB218. (Wright & Logan)

Motor Torpedo Boats 73, 74, 75, 76, 77, 78, 79, 80, 81, 82, 83, 84, 85, 86, 87, 88, 89, 90, 91, 92, 93, 94, 95, 96, 97 and 98

Built 1941–1942

Displacement tons	47
Dimensions	72½ x 19¼ x 3¾/5½
Armament	Two .5in mg, four .303in mg
Torpedo tubes	Two 21in
Machinery	Three shaft petrol engines, 4,050/3,600bhp
Speed	40/38 knots
Complement	12

Losses: HM MTB80 was lost in 1943 (date, cause and place not known).

HM MTB74 was engaged in the raid on St Nazaire and sank from gunfire of German shore batteries on 28 March 1942.

HM MTB87 was mined in the North Sea on 31 October 1942.

HM MTB73 was attacked by German aircraft on 24 December 1943 off Maddalena.

HM MTB77 was attacked by German aircraft off Vito Valencia on 8 September 1943.

HM MTB93 was lost after collision with HM MTB729 off Harwich on 18 August 1944.

Built by Vosper (Portsmouth).

MTB73. (Vosper Thornycroft)

MTB97. (Vosper Thornycroft)

Motor Torpedo Boats 222, 223, 224, 225, 226, 227, 228, 229, 230, 231, 232, 233, 234, 235, 236, 237, 238, 239, 240, 241, 242, 243, 244 and 245

Built 1942

Specification

Displacement tons	47
Dimensions	72½ x 19¼ x 2¾/5½
Armament	One 20mm, two .5in mg
Torpedo tubes	Two 21in
Machinery	Three shaft petrol engines, 4,050/3,600bhp
Speed	39½/34 knots
Complement	13

Note: Many of these boats were used for minelaying.

Losses: HM MTB222 (R Neth N *Sperwer*) was mined in the North Sea on 10 November 1943.

HM MTB230 was lost in collision with HM MTB222 in the North Sea on 9 November 1943.

HM MTB237 was sunk in a surface action when off Barfleur on 7 August 1942.

HM MTB241 was sunk in a surface action when off Ijmuiden on 31 March 1944.

HM MTB242 foundered while in tow for Malta in May 1945.

HM MTB243 was expended as a target by own forces while off Malta in July 1945.

Built by Vosper (Portsmouth).

MTB224. (Imperial War Museum)

Motor Torpedo Boats 347, 348, 349, 350, 351, 352, 353, 354, 355, 356, 357, 358, 359, 360, 361 and 362

All built 1943

Specification

Displacement tons	45
Dimensions	72½ x 19¼ x 2¾/5½
Armament	One 20mm, three .5in mg, four .303in mg, but in some boats the .5in were replaced with a further 20mm single and in others the forward 20mm was exchanged for a 1pdr
Torpedo tubes	Two 21in
Machinery	Three shaft petrol engines, 4,050/3,600bhp
Speed	39½/35 knots
Complement	12

Losses: HM MTB347 was sunk in a surface action when off Ijmuiden on 1 October 1944.

HM MTB352 collided with an unknown vessel on 26 March 1944 in the North Sea.

HM MTB356 was sunk in surface action when off Ijmuiden on 16 October 1943, likewise No.360 on 1 October 1944.

HM MTB357 while engaged in a surface action with German light forces off the Dutch coast, was severely damaged by gunfire on 23 December 1943, and foundered the following day.

MTB347. (Vosper Thornycroft)

MTB355. (Vosper Thornycroft)

MTBs 347, 348 and 349 were built by Vosper (Portchester) and 351, 352, 353 and 354 by Vosper (Wivenhoe), 350 and 355 to 359 by Harland & Wolff, and 360, 361 and 362 by Morgan Giles (Teignmouth).

Motor Torpedo Boats 380, 381, 382, 383, 384, 385, 386, 387, 388, 389, 390, 391, 392 393, 391, and 395

Built 1941

Specification

Displacement tons	44½
Dimensions	73 x 19½ x 2¾ x 5½
Armament	Two 20mm, two .5in mg, four .303in mg
Torpedo tubes	Four 18in
Machinery	Three shaft petrol engines 4,050/3,600bhp
Speed	39½/34 knots
Complement	13

All built by Vosper (Portsmouth).

MTB380. (Vosper Thornycroft)

MTB385. (Vosper Thornycroft)

Motor Torpedo Boats 523, 524, 525, 526, 527, 528, 529, 530, 531, 532, 533, 534, 535, 536 and 537

Built 1944–1945, but see cancellation note below

Specification

Displacement tons	48
Dimensions	72½ x 19½ x 5½
Armament	One 6pdr, two 20mm, four .303in mg
Torpedo tubes	Two 21in
Machinery	Three shaft petrol engines, 4,050bhp
Speed	40/38 knots
Complement	13

Cancellation note: Boats 534, 535 and 536 being built at the yard of Vosper (Portsmouth) were cancelled.

Built by Vosper (Portsmouth).

MTB525. (World Ship Society)

MTB530. (Wright & Logan)

J.S. White & Co. Motor Torpedo Boats

Motor Torpedo Boats 41, 42, 43, 44, 45, 46, 47, 48, 201, 203, 204, 205, 206, 207, 208, 209, 210, 211, 212, 246, 247, 248, 249, 250, 251, 252, 253, 254, 255, 256 and 257

Built 1940–1943

Specification

Displacement tons	33 for boats 41–48, 38½ tons for boats 201–212, 41 tons for boats 246–257
Dimensions	73 x 18 x 2¾/5½
Armament	Two .5in mg, two .303in mg
Torpedo tubes	Two 21in
Machinery	Three shaft petrol engines, 3,360 bhp
Speed	39¾/33½ knots
Complement	12

Losses: HM MTB41 was mined in the North Sea on 14 February 1941.
HM MTB43 sank after a surface action with German Naval Forces off Gravelines on 18 August 1942
HM MTB44 sank after a surface action with German Naval Forces off Dover on 7 August 1942.
HM MTB47 sank after surface action with German Naval Forces off Cape Gris nez on 17 January 1942
HM MTB203 (as R Neth N *Arend*) lost by unknown cause off Dover in May 1944.
HM MTB248 was in collision in the English Channel on 6 June 1944.
HM MTB255 caught fire at Ostend on 14 February 1945.
Built by White (Cowes).

Motor Torpedo Boats 424, 425, 426, 427, 428 and 429

All built 1944

Specification

Displacement tons	46¾
Dimensions	73 x 18 x 2¾/5½
Armament	One 6pdr, two 20mm, four .303in mg
Torpedo tubes	Two 18in
Machinery	Three shaft petrol engines, 3,360bhp
Speed	39¾/33¼ knots
Complement	17

Built by White (Cowes).

Right: MTB45. (Imperial War Museum)

Below: MTB48. (Imperial War Museum)

Below, bottom: MTB426. (Source not known)

Ex-American 'PT' Type Motor Torpedo Boats

Motor Torpedo Boats 259, 260, 261, 262, 263, 264, 265, 266 and 267

All supplied under Lease Lend 1941–1942 but built 1940

Specification

Displacement tons	32
Dimensions	70 x 20 x 4
Armament	Four .5in mg
Torpedo tubes	Four 18in
Machinery	Three shaft petrol engines, 4,050/3,600bhp
Speed	45/40 knots
Complement	12

Note: HM MTB267 for a short time was converted for minelaying and carried four mines.

Losses: HM MTB259 foundered in tow in the Mediterranean on 14 June 1942.

HM MTB262 was lost, cause unknown, in the Mediterranean in February 1943.

HM MTB261 was lost, cause unknown, when off Alexandria on 26 August 1945.

HM MTB264 was mined off Sousse on 10 May 1943.

HM MTB267 foundered in heavy weather, between Benghazi and Malta on 2 April 1943.

Built by Electric Boat Co. (Bayonne).

Motor Torpedo Boats 307, 308, 309, 310, 311, 312, 313, 314, 315, 316, 317, 318, 319, 320, 321, 322, 323, 324, 325 and 326

Ex-US Navy PT 49–56 and 57–68, the latter being designated PTC
All PT boats and similar were supplied under Lease Lend
Built 1942

Specification

Displacement tons	45
Dimensions	77 x 20 x 5½
Armament	One 20mm, four .5in mg
Torpedo tubes	Two 21in
Machinery	Three shaft petrol engines, 4,050/3,600bhp
Speed	45/40 knots
Complement	12

Losses: HM MTBs 308 and 310 were lost after aircraft attack on 14 September 1942 at Tobruk.

HM MTB311 was mined off Malta on 2 May 1943.

HM MTB312 was lost after aircraft attack on 14 September 1942 at Tobruk.

MTB307. (World Ship Society)

HM MTB314 was at Tobruk on 14 September 1942 and was bombed and
beached. Later salvaged by German forces, becoming the German RA10, but was
attacked by British aircraft on 30 April 1943 and sank.

HM MTB316 sank during an unequal surface action with the Italian cruiser
Scipione off Reggio on 17 July 1943.

Built by Electric Boat Co. (Bayonne).

Motor Torpedo Boats 419, 420, 421, 422 and 423

Ex-USN PT Boats
Built 1942

Specification

Displacement tons	35
Dimensions	81 x 20 x 6
Armament	One 40mm, one 20mm, four .5in mg
Torpedo tubes	Two 21in
Machinery	Three shaft petrol engines 4,050bhp
Speed	40 knots
Complement	12

Built by Higgins (New Orleans).
Initials: PT boat is the United States Navy equivalent of MTB in the Royal Navy.
PTC boat is the United States Navy equivalent of MA/SB in the Royal Navy.

Ex-American Motor Torpedo Boats

Motor Torpedo Boats 269, 270, 271, 272, 273 and 274

Ex-PT Boats in service with the US Navy, previously numbered PT 5–8, 3 and 4

PT6(II) was the second of this number, PT6(I) having been delivered to the RN as an MGB

Dimensions and displacement   PT3 and 4 were 59ft and of 25 tons, PT5, 6, 7 and 8 were 81ft and of 34 tons, and the latter two were of aluminium construction.

Other details as PT49 (HM MTB307).

Boats 269 and 270 were built by Higgins (New Orleans). 271 and 272 by Philadelphia Navy Yard. 273 and 274 by Fisher Boat Works (Detroit).

Motor Torpedo Boat 258

Built 1939

Specification

Displacement tons	30
Dimensions	70 x 20 x 4
Armament	Four .5in mg
Torpedo tubes	Four 18in
Machinery	Three shaft petrol engines, 3,300/3,000bhp
Speed	44½/40 knots
Complement	12

MTB258. (Source not known)

Note: This Motor Torpedo Boat was built by the British Power Boat Co. (Hythe) in 1939 as a private venture, but was not accepted by the Royal Navy. Consequently, the craft was offered to the United States Navy and became their PT9. It was used as the prototype of all PT boat development. Under Lease Lend she was returned to this country in 1941 and became HM MTB258.

Motor Torpedo Boats 275, 276, 277, 278, 279, 280, 281, 282, 283, 284, 285, 286, 287, 288, 289, 290, 291, 292, 293, 294, 295, 296, 297, 298, 299, 300. 301, 302, 303, 304, 305, 306, 363, 364, 365, 366, 367, 368, 369, 370, 371, 372, 373, 374, 375, 376, 377, 378, 396, 397, 398, 399, 400, 401, 402, 403, 405, 406, 407, 408, 409, 410 and 411

Built 1942–1944

Specification

Displacement tons	37
Dimensions	72½ x 19¼ x 2/6¼
Armament	One 20mm, two .5in mg (some boats were fitted with a twin 20mm in lieu of the .5in mg)
Torpedo tubes	Two 21in
Machinery	Three shaft petrol engines, 4,050/3,600bhp
Speed	39½/35 knots
Complement	13

Note: All built for Vospers in the United States and became USNs BPT 21–28, 49–52, 29–48, 53–68 and PT384–399, all being transferred to the RN under Lease Lend.

Losses: HM MTBs 284 and 285 were deck cargo on the SS *Larchbank* which sank south of Italy on 9 September 1943.

HM MTB288 was bombed on 22 July 1943 by German aircraft at Augusta.

HM MTB287 went aground on Levrera Island in the Adriatic and was blown up on 24 November 1944.

HM MTB371 went ashore on 24 November 1944 in the Adriatic and was blown up.

HM MTB372 was lost from gunfire of German surface craft in the Northern Adriatic on 24 July 1944.

Boats 275–282 and 363–378 were built by Annapolis Yacht Yard, 297–306 were built by Harbour Boat Building (Terminal Island), 283–290 were built by Herreshoff Mfg Co. (Bristol) and 291–296 and 396–411 were built by Philadelphia Navy Yard.

Ex-Canadian Motor Torpedo Boats

Motor Torpedo Boats 332, 333, 334, 335, 336, 337, 338, 339, 340, 341, 342 and 343

Built 1941

Specification

Displacement tons	32
Dimensions	70 x 20 x 4
Armament	Four .5in mg
Torpedo tubes	Four 18in
Machinery	Three shaft petrol engines, 4,050bhp
Speed	45/40 knots
Complement	12

Note: Built to a design of the British Power Boat Co. based on one of their 70ft MTBs sold to the Royal Canadian Navy in 1939 and commissioned as CMTB1.

Loss: HM MTB338 caught fire at Trinidad on 16 May 1942.

Built by Canadian Power Boat Co. (Montreal).

Ex-Chinese Motor Torpedo Boats

Motor Torpedo Boats 26 and 27

Built, 1938

Specification

Displacement tons	13¾
Dimensions	55 x 11 x 3¼
Armament	Two .303in mg
Torpedoes	Two 18in in troughs
Machinery	Two shaft petrol engines, 1,200bhp
Speed	40 knots
Complement	5

Note: These pre–Second World War MTBs were built for, and acquired from, the Chinese Navy.

Losses: HM MTB26 was lost from gunfire of Japanese landing craft at Hong Kong on 19 December 1941.

    HM MTB27 was scuttled by own forces at Hong Kong on 26 December 1941.

Built by Thornycroft (Hampton).

Ex-Finnish Motor Torpedo Boats

Motor Torpedo Boats 67 and 68

Built 1940–1941

Specification

Displacement tons	17
Dimensions	55 x 11 x 3¼
Armament	Four .303in mg
Torpedoes	Two 18in in troughs
Machinery	Two shaft petrol engines, 1,200bhp
Speed	40 knots
Complement	5

Note: These two MTBs were building at Thornycroft's Yard for the Finnish Navy but were taken over by the Admiralty.

Losses: HM MTB67 was bombed by aircraft at Suda Bay on 23 May 1941.
HM MTB68 was in collision with MTB215 and later sank off the Libyan coast on 14 December 1941.

Built by Thornycroft (Hampton).

Ex-Greek Motor Torpedo Boats

Motor Torpedo Boats 69 and 70

Specification

Displacement tons	35
Dimensions	70 x 14¾ x 3¼/5
Armament	Ten .303in mg, two 'dustbins' and two singles
Torpedo tubes	Two 21in
Machinery	Two shaft petrol engines, 2,300bhp
Speed	27½ knots
Complement	10

Note: Originally designed for three shafts/engines but due to the shortage of Italian IF engines, only two engines were fitted.

Construction note: These Motor Torpedo Boats were under construction at Vosper's Yard for the Greek Navy but were taken over by the Admiralty. They would have been named T3 and T4. The Greek Government re-ordered four boats – T3–T6 –, but with the fall of Greece they were again taken over by the Admiralty.

Built by Vosper (Portsmouth).

MTB70. (Vosper Thornycroft)

MTB72. (Vosper Thornycroft)

Ex-Norwegian Motor Torpedo Boats

Motor Torpedo Boats 71 and 72

Built 1940

Specification

Displacement tons	25
Dimensions	60 x 15 x 3½
Armament	Two .5in mg
Torpedo tubes	Two 18in
Machinery	Two shaft petrol engines, 2,200bhp
Speed	35 knots
Complement	10

Note: These were two of four MTBs being built for the Royal Norwegian Navy. The first two – nos 5 and 6 – were delivered and lost in their service, but the latter pair nos – 7 and 8 – were taken over by the Admiralty.

Built by Vosper (Portsmouth).

Ex-Philippines Motor Torpedo Boats

Motor Torpedo Boats 327, 328, 329, 330 and 331

Built 1940–1941

Specification

Displacement tons	17
Dimensions	55 x 11 x 3¼
Armament	Four .303in mg
Torpedoes	Two 18in in troughs
Machinery	Two shaft petrol engines, 1,200bhp
Speed	40 knots
Complement	5

Note: These MTBs were building at Thornycroft's Yard for the Philippines Navy but were taken over by the Admiralty.
Built by Thornycroft (Hampton).

Motor Torpedo Boats Experimental Boats

Motor Torpedo Boat 100

Built 1939

Specification

Displacement tons	22
Dimensions	60¼ x 13¼ x 3
Armament	Eight .303in mg
Torpedo tubes	Two 18in
Machinery	Two shaft petrol engines, 1,500bhp
Speed	25 knots
Complement	9

Note: Was designed and built as Motor Minesweeper 51 by the British Power Boat Co. but was not a success, hence being converted to a Motor Torpedo Boat.

Motor Torpedo Boat 101

Built 1939

Specification

Displacement tons	22
Dimensions	67¼ x 14½ x 3
Armament	Two 20mm

MMS551, later MTB100. (Wright & Logan)

MTB100. (Wright & Logan)

Torpedo tubes	Two 21in
Machinery	Three shaft petrol engines, 3,450/300bhp
Speed	42/36 knots

Note: This was a private venture with Admiralty approval. HM MTB101 was built as a hydrofoil (see HMS *Speedy,* page 240) and became an operational boat.

Loss: HM MTB101 was lost in 1942 through hydrofoil failure.

Built by J.S. White & Co.

Motor Torpedo Boat 102

Built 1937

Specification

Displacement tons	32
Dimensions	68 x 14¾ x 3¼
Armament	One 20mm
Torpedo tubes	Two 21in
Machinery	Three shaft petrol engines, 3,450/3,000bhp
Speed	43½/35½ knots
Complement	10

Note: Built by Vospers as a private speculation and was originally fitted with a bow torpedo tube in the hull and a reload carried on deck.

MTB102. (Wright & Logan)

Motor Torpedo Boat 103

Built 1940 as a private venture by Vosper's with a stepped hull, similar to Thornycroft
  CMBs of the Second World War, but the Italian engines for MTB 103 were never
  delivered and she was completed as Target Boat CT05.

Motor Torpedo Boat 104, 105, 106 and 107

Built 1940 by Thornycroft

MTB 104 was 50ft, 105 and 106 were 45½ft and of 9 tons (CMB Type) and 107 was of
  44¼ft.

Losses: HM MTB106 was mined in the Thames Estuary on 16 October 1940.
  HM MTB105 was hung in davits on HMS *Fidelity* and, when the latter sank, 105
  floated off but was sunk by HMCS *Woodstock* in the English Channel on 1 January
  1943.

HM MTB108

Built 1940, was a 45ft hydroplane, lost incomplete in 1940 at Vosper's Yard.

HM MTB109

Built by McGrue Boats Ltd, was of 17 tons and 41 x 11 x 2¾ dimensions, but was never
  completed for operations.

HM MTBs 344, 345 and 346

Built 1943

These were boats with stepped hulls, 344 was 60ft and 345 and 346 were 45ft.
All twin screw with engines of 1200bhp giving 40 knots, the armament was two 18in
  torpedoes in troughs.

Loss: HM MTB345 when in the service of the Royal Norwegian Navy was lost at
  Aspoy after catching fire on 28 July 1943.
Built by Thornycroft.

Motor Torpedo Boat 379

This was the prototype MTB for the series commencing 380 by Vospers, introduced on
  this craft was a flush decked hull, manual twin 20mm mounting and four torpedoes.

MTB103. (Wright & Logan)

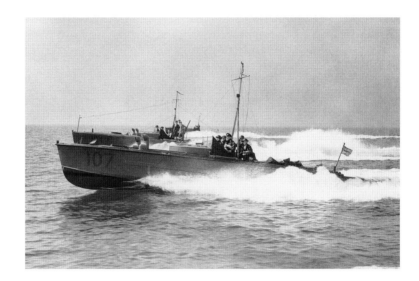

MTBs 104 and 107. (Imperial War Museum)

MTB344. (National Maritime Museum)

Motor Torpedo Boat 501

Built 1942 but completed as an MGB by Camper & Nicholson.

Motor Torpedo Boat 510

Built 1943 and completed as an MGB by Vosper Ltd.

For particulars of HM MTBs 501 and 510 see HM MGBs 501 and 510 (page 122).

Motor Torpedo Boat 538

Built 1948

Specification

Displacement tons	36
Dimensions	74½ x 20¼ x 6
Armament (as MTB)	Two 20mm, four 18in tubes
Armament (as MGB)	One short 4.5in, two 20mm
Machinery	Three shaft petrol engines, 4,050bhp
Speed	40/31 knots
Complement	15

Note: Built by Vosper's as an interchangeable MTB/MGB and completed as an MGB but was then re-named MTB1601.

MTB538. (P.A. Vicary)

Motor Torpedo Boat 539

Built 1950

Specification

Displacement tons	43
Dimensions	75¼ x 19¾ x 5½
Armament	One 6pdr, one 20mm
Torpedo tubes	Four 18in
Machinery	Three shaft petrol engines, 4,050bhp
Speed	42/35 knots
Complement	16

Note: This was the prototype of the 'Dark' Class interchangeable MTB/MGBs and was of alloy construction. She was re-named MTB1602.
Built by Saunders Roe (Anglesey) Ltd.

HMS *Bloodhound* Motor Torpedo Boat

HMS	Completed	Builder
Bloodhound	1937	Vosper

Specification

Displacement tons	35
Dimensions	68 x 19 x 3
Torpedo Armament	One 21in
Machinery	Two shaft petrol engines, 1,600bhp
Speed	25 knots
Complement	6

Bloodhound.
(Vosper Ltd)

Note: Was built for use as a tender to HMS *Vernon*.

Loss: HMS *Bloodhound* was wrecked in January 1943 at Bincleaves.

HMS *Tarret* Motor Torpedo Boat

Little is known of this Motor Torpedo Boat excepting that she was built of steel for the
Admiralty and completed in 1940

Specification

Length	100ft
Machinery	Diesel engines to twin shafts
Speed	30 knots

Note: HMS *Tarret* was designed as a Motor Torpedo Boat but entered service as a Motor
Anti-submarine Boat, being later used for training.

Built by Swan Hunter & Wigham Richardson.

Tarret. (Swan Hunter)

Chapter 12

Miscellaneous Coastal Craft

Ex-Italian Motor Torpedo Boat

Specification (as built)

Displacement tons	20
Dimensions	69 x 14¾ x 4½
Armament	One 13.2mm mg
Torpedoes	Two 17.7in side launched
Anti-submarine	Six depth charges
Machinery	Two shaft petrol engines, 2,000hp
Speed	40 knots plus
Range	200nm
Complement	10

Note: This Motor Torpedo Boat was captured on 27 July 1941 off Malta being the ex-Italian MAS452. She was taken into service by the Royal Navy and officially known as HMS *Xmas*.

This craft was built in February 1941 by Baglietto Varaxze.

Xmas. (Fototeca)

Ex-American Coastal Transports

Coastal Transports FT1, FT2, FT3, FT4, FT5, FT6, FT7, FT8, FT9, FT10, FT11, FT12, FT13, FT14, FT15, FT16, FT17, FT18, FT19, FT20, FT21, FT22, FT23, FT25, FT26, FT27, FT28, FT29 and FT30

Built 1943

Specification

Displacement tons	238
Dimensions	110 x 21¼ x 11
Armament	Four 20mm
Machinery	One shaft diesel engine, 400bhp
Complement	20

Note: All built in the United States and transferred to the Royal Navy under the Lease Lend agreement.

Their USN numbers had been APC 51–56, 58–61, 65–66, 71–72, 75–79, 62–64, 67–70, 73–74 and 97.

Builders

Bristol Yacht Co.	FT13–14, FT28–29
Camden Shipbuilding	FT7–10, FT21–23
Hogden Bros	FT11–12, FT24–27
H.C. Marr (Damariscotta)	FT5–6 and 20
Noank Shipbuilding	FT30
W.A. Robinson (Ipswich)	FT15–19
Warren Boats	FT1–4

FT25. (Source not known)

Australian General Purpose Vessels

HMAS/HMS	Completed	Transferred to Royal Navy	Builder
GPV954	1945	1951	Green Point Shipyard
GPV956	1945	1951	Green Point Shipyard
GPV959	1945	1951	Green Point Shipyard
GPV963	1945	1952	Green Point Shipyard

Specification

Displacement (Standard)	77
Dimensions	75¼ x 19¼ x 7¼
Armament	One 20mm DP/AA plus small arms
Machinery	One single shaft diesel engine giving 160bhp
Speed	8 knots
Range	900nm at 8 knots
Complement	12 plus

Notes: These GPVs were designed and built for the Royal Australian Navy to be used as craft for harbour and anchorage support services. When transferred to the Royal Navy post-war during the Malayan Emergency, the four craft were designated as the 209th Minesweeping Flotilla but their employment is uncertain as they were also described as 'tenders to HMS *Terror*'. The design was similar to the 75ft Admiralty Motor Fishing vessels of the Second World War.

GPV961. (Australian War Memorial)

Chapter 13

'P' Class Motor Launches

HMS	Completed	Builder
Pahlawan (later ML1102)	1939	Thornycroft (Singapore)
Panglima (later ML1103)	1939	Thornycroft (Singapore)
Panji	1939	Thornycroft (Singapore)
Peningat (later ML1104)	1939	Thornycroft (Singapore)

Specification

Displacement tons	60
Dimensions	76½ x 13½ x 4¾
Armament	One 3pdr, one .303in mg
Machinery	Three shaft petrol and diesel engines, 780bhp
Speed	16 knots
Complement	10

Note: These MLs had a minesweeping capability.

All built for use by the Royal Naval Volunteer Reserve Division at Singapore.

Loss: HMS *Peningat* was lost on the occupation of Singapore by Japanese forces in December 1942.

Peningat.
(Imperial War Museum)

Chapter 14

Fairmile 'A', 'B', 'C', 'D' and 'F' Type Motor Launches

Fairmile 'A' Type Motor Launch

HM ML	Completed	Builder
100	1940	Woodnutt (St Helens)
101	1940	Macraft (Sarnia)
102	1940	Woodnutt (St Helens)
103	1940	Brooke Marine (Lowestoft)
104	1940	Dickie (Bangor)
105	1940	Macraft (Sarnia)
106	1940	Grew Boats
107	1940	Grew Boats
108	1940	Midland Boat Works
109	1940	Wm Osborne (Littlehampton)
110	1940	Minette Shields (Bracebridge)
111	1940	Le Blanc SB (Weymouth)

'A' type Fairmile. (Imperial War Museum)

Specification

Displacement tons	60
Dimensions	110 x 17½ x 4½/6½
Armament	One 3pdr, two .303in mg
Anti-submarine	Twelve depth charges
Machinery	Three shaft petrol engines, 1,800bhp
Speed	25 knots
Complement	16

Note: All of these MLs were converted to minelayers with an alternative armament of three 20mm in lieu of the .303in mg. Minelaying capacity was nine contact or six ground mines.

Losses: HM ML103 was mined in the Dover Straits on 24 August 1942.

HM ML108 was mined in the English Channel on 5 September 1943.

HM ML109 was mined in the Humber estuary on 30 October 1940.

HM ML111 was mined off the Humber Light Vessel on 25 November 1940.

Fairmile 'B' Type Motor Launch

Motor Launches 112–311, 336–500, 511–600, 801–933, 4001–4004, 050–129 (ex-001–080)

All built 1940 to 1944 inclusive

Specification

Displacement tons	65 to No.123, 73 thereafter 103, 145, 511
Dimensions	112 x 18¼ x 3¾/4¾
Armament	One 3pdr and two .303in mg
Anti-submarine	Up to twelve depth charges
Machinery	Two shaft petrol engines 1,200bhp
Speed	20/16¾ knots
Complement	16

Note: The 'B' MLs were used in many operations as Rescue MLs, Ambulance MLs, Minesweeping MLs and Minelaying MLs. In 1940 some were armed with two 21in torpedo tubes as anti-invasion attack craft. They sustained many losses, as listed below.

Losses: HM ML130 was sunk in action by Italian surface craft off Malta on 7 May 1942.

HM ML132, while on patrol off Bone was taken by the enemy on 22 March 1942.

HM ML133 on 11 May 1943 was lost by fire in Scottish waters.

HM ML126 was torpedoed by a U-boat off the west coast of Italy on 27 November 1914.

HM ML127 on 22 November 1940 was mined in the Thames estuary.

HM ML129 was lost in a surface action with Italian craft off Cape Bon on 22 March 1942.

ML103.
(Imperial War
Museum)

ML145.
(Imperial War
Museum)

Rescue
ML511. (Wright
& Logan)

HM ML267, when Free French-manned, was lost by damage from shore batteries at St Nazaire on 28 March 1942, likewise ML268 and ML270, except that the latter was sunk by own forces that same day.

HM ML298 as ML268.

HM ML306 was damaged by shore batteries at St Nazaire on 28 March 1942 and abandoned. She was later recovered and recommissioned by the German Navy as RA9, and on 16 August 1944 was attacked by Allied aircraft off Le Havre and sank.

HM MLs 446, 447 and 457 as ML268.

HM ML144 on 22 September 1941 was mined off Dungeness.

HM ML156 on 28 March 1942 during the raid on St Nazaire was severely damaged by German shore batteries and later sunk by own forces.

HM ML160 was bombed by German aircraft while in Brixham Harbour on 6 May 1942.

HM ML169, while at Gibraltar, was lost by fire on 15 February 1942.

HM ML177 was severely damaged during the raid at St Nazaire by German shore batteries on 28 March 1942.

HM ML183 whilst manoeuvring in Dieppe Harbour on 11 February 1945, was lost by collision.

HM ML192 was severely damaged during the raid on St Nazaire by German shore batteries on 28 March 1942.

HM ML210 was mined off Dieppe on 15 February 1944.

HM ML216 was mined in the North Sea on 19 September 1944 and later foundered on 28 September 1944.

HM ML219 was wrecked off Stornowaywhilst on passage in bad weather on 21 November 1941.

HM ML230 was in collision off the coast of Ceylon on 17 August 1945.

HM ML242 was lost by fire while in Freetown Harbour on 29 November 1942.

HM ML251 was in collision with an unknown vessel while off the Gambia River on 6 March 1943.

HM ML258 was mined off Rimini on 16 September 1944.

HM ML262 was severely damaged by German shore batteries during the raid on St Nazaire on 28 March 1942.

HM ML265 was lost by fire while in Freetown Harbour on 1 July 1944.

HM ML287 was lost by fire while in Freetown Harbour on 1 July 1944.

HM ML288 foundered off West Hartlepool in bad weather on 11 October 1941.

HM ML301 was lost by fire while in Freetown Harbour on 9 August 1942.

HM ML310 was lost during a surface action with Japanese forces off Tjebia Island on 15 February 1942.

HM ML311 was lost during a surface action with Japanese forces off the Banka Strait on 14 February 1942.

HM ML339 was torpedoed by an E-boat in the North Sea on 7 October 1942.

HM MLs 352 and 353 were lost after an attack by German aircraft on Tobruk Harbour on 14 September 1942.

HM ML358 was lost in surface action off Leros on 12 November 1943.

HM ML387 was destroyed by fire in Beirut Harbour on 5 March 1944.

HM ML443 was mined off Vada on 12 July 1944.

HM ML444 was lost by fire at Maddalena on 22 May 1944.

HM ML466 was mined off the Island of Waicheren on 25 March 1945.

HM ML562 sank off Ischia on 31 October 1944, after an engagement with shore batteries.

HM ML563 was mined off Frejus on 16 August 1941.

HM ML579 was bombed on 12 October 1943 by German aircraft at Leros.

HM ML591 took the ground and later sank in the Sittang river on 9 May 1945.

HM ML835 was bombed on 12 October 1943 by German aircraft at Leros.

HM ML870 was mined off Piraeus on 15 October 1944.

HM ML147 became a constructive total loss off Portsmouth on 3 November 1944.

HM ML385 caught fire and became a constructive total loss off Alexandria in 1944.

HM ML460 became a constructive total loss off Malta on 2 April 1945.

HM ML890 was mined off Ramree Island on 21 January 1945.

HM ML905 took the ground and later sank on 9 May 1945 in the Sittang River

HM ML916 was mined off Walsoorden on 8 November 1944.

MLs 362, 363, 364, 365, 372, 373, 374, 375, 432 and 433 were destroyed by own forces while building in the face of the Japanese advance at Singapore in February 1942.

MLs 376 and 377 were destroyed on the stocks at Hong Kong in the face of the Japanese advance in December 1941.

MLs 436 and 437 were destroyed on the stocks at Rangoon in April 1942 in the face of the Japanese advance.

Transfers: HM MLs 050–129 to the RCN, 829–832 and 848–857 to the SANF, HM MLs 390–391, 412–423, and 436–441 to the RIM.

HM MLs 400–411 to the RNZN, 424–431 and 801–827 to the RAN. HM MLs 138, 143, 162 and 164 to the R Neth N.

HM MLs 123, 182, 205, 245–247, 267–269, 303, 244, 271, 266, 302, 052, 052, 062 and 063 to the Free French.

Builders (Craft built in the UK)

Aldous Successors (Brightlingsea): Nos 138, 170, 206, 225, 278, 301, 463, 492, 519, 559.

Austin's (East Ham): Nos 227, 287, 450, 482, 514, 542, 549, 570, 925, 933.

Boat Construction Co. (Falmouth): Nos 137, 164, 181, 226, 261, 271, 336, 446, 471,491.

Brooke Marine (Oulton Broad): Nos 114, 127, 142, 147, 186, 211, 230, 248, 270, 281, 290, 344, 443, 527, 562.

Cardnell Bros (Maylandsea): Nos 215, 288, 461, 534.

Collins (Lowestoft): Nos 180, 262, 341, 479, 515, 541, 569, 926.

Curtis (Looe): Nos 123, 130, 131, 139, 140,143, 145, 146, 161, 172, 173, 174, 241, 242, 249, 250, 251, 256, 257, 276 (Par), 280, 295, 307, 308, 458, 465,480, 481, 490, 493, 513,521, 525, 530, 533 566, 568.

Dickie (Bangor): Nos 122, 162, 183, 212, 235, 460, 500, 537, 565.

Dickie (Tarbert): Nos 124, 188, 217, 234, 337.

Diesel Constructors (Isleworth): No.345.

HM Dockyard (Sheerness): Nos 150, 151, 245, 246.

Doig (Grimsbv): Nos 125, 222, 286, 464, 512.

Dorset Yacht (Hamworthy): Nos 135, 144, 189, 229, 258, 268, 293, 296, 298, 462.

Harris (Appledore): Nos 128, 152, 184, 233, 263, 279, 303, 450, 451.

Itchenor Shipyard: Nos 132, 191, 282, 466, 524, 558, 913.

Johnson & Jago (Leigh-on-Sea): Nos 194, 207, 264, 274, 305, 342, 457, 469, 486, 487, 522, 532, 543, 548, 564, 572, 575, 577, 580, 581, 584, 587, 590, 593, 597, 901, 903, 907, 909, 911, 915, 918, 923.

Wm King (Burnham-on-Crouch): 169, 221, 226, 302.

Kris Cruisers (Isleworth): No.165.

Lady Bee (Southwick): No.117.

Mashford Bros (Cremyll): Nos 129, 141, 213, 255, 292, 452.

Jas. Miller (St Monance): Nos 108, 126, 159, 196, 203, 303, 313, 346, 483, 489, 518, 529, 546, 552, 573, 574, 578, 579, 585, 586, 592, 598, 902, 904, 910, 914, 919, 924, 928.

Wm Osborne (Littlehampton): Nos 175, 210, 219, 273, 291.

H.J. Percival (Horning): Nos 153, 193, 244, 283, 447, 470, 523, 531, 567, 917.

Alex-Robertson (Sandbank): Nos 136, 160, 197, 223, 238, 454.

Leo Robertson (Oulton Broad): Nos 163, 178, 182, 259, 340 (Tewkesbury), 258.

J. Sadd (Maldon): Nos 181, 253, 294, 456, 517.

Jas. Silver (Rosneath): Nos 200, 201, 232, 284.

Solent Shipyard (Salisbury Green): Nos 134, 177, 190, 239, 267, 285, 306, 459, 472, 526, 563.

Southampton Seam Joinery: No.252.

Sussex Sbdg (Shoreham): Nos 133, 148, 202, 216, 231, 299, 488, 496.

Jas. Taylor (Chertsey): Nos 185, 205, 209, 453, 520, 571, 576, 588, 905, 908, 922.

Thomson & Balfour (Bo'ness): Nos 240, 275, 478, 494.

Thornycroft (Hampton): Nos 157, 195, 260, 343.

Tough Bros (Teddington): Nos 113, 171, 199, 220, 228, 448.

J.W.&A. Upham (Brixham): Nos 166, 167, 179, 236, 237, 247, 254, 277, 297, 309, 445, 511.

Wallasea Bay Yacht Stn: Nos 224, 272, 289, 339.

Wm Weatherhead (Cockenzie): Nos 168, 218, 243, 269, 300, 455, 473, 495, 516, 535

Woodnut

    (St Helen's): Nos 112, 155, 198.

    (Portsmouth): No.149.

    (Dumbarton): Nos 121, 154, 176.

    (Rochford): No.156.

    (Southampton): Nos 158, 192, 208, 265, 338, 449, 467, 468, 497.

    (Northam): Nos 204, 498, 499.

    (Blyth): No.214.

Builders unknown: Nos 115, 116, 118, 119, 120, 347, 444, 484, 485, 536, 538, 539, 540, 544, 545, 547, 551, 553, 554, 555, 556, 557, 560, 561, 582, 583, 589, 591, 594, 595, 596, 599, 600, 906, 912, 916, 920, 921, 927, 929, 930, 931, 932.

Builders (Craft built abroad)

Anglo-American Nile Tourist Co. (Cairo): Nos 360, 361, 386, 387, 835, 836.

Assoc. Boat Bldr (Auckland): Nos 403, 404, 405, 406.

Bailey (Auckland): Nos 400, 401, 402.

Belmont Dock (Jamaica): Nos 378, 379, 422, 423, 858, 859.

A.C. Benson (Vancouver): Nos 068, 069, 128, 129.

C.L. Burland (Bermuda): Nos 368, 369, 370, 371.

Burn & Co. (Calcutta): No.441.

Thos. Cook (Cairo): Nos 384, 385.

Garden Reach (Calcutta): Nos 412, 413, 414, 415, 418, 439, 440, 477.

Greavette Boats (Gravenhurst): Nos 054, 055, 056, 077, 078, 114.

Green Point Boatyard (Sydney): Nos 424, 425, 426, 427, 428, 429, 430, 431, 801, 802, 803, 804, 805, 806, 807, 808, 809, 810, 811, 812.

Grew Boats (Penatanguishene): Nos 072, 073, 098, 099, 100, 106, 107, 117.

Halvorsen (Sydney): Nos 813, 814, 817, 818, 819, 820, 821, 822, 823, 824, 825.

Hunter Boats (Orillia): Nos 060, 061,085, 092, 093, 109, 116.

Indian General Nav. & Rly. Co. (Calcutta): Nos 438, 474, 475, 476.

Le Blanc Sbdg (Weymouth): Nos 064, 065, 083, 084, 120, 121.

Louw & Halvorsen (Capetown): Nos 383, 829, 830, 831, 832, 846, 847, 854, 855.

MacCraft (Sarnia): Nos 062, 063, 115.

Midland Boat Works: Nos 050, 051, 081, 082, 094, 095, 118.

Minette Shields (Bracebridge): Nos 057, 058, 059, 074, 075, 076, 096, 097, 110, 119.

H. Mahatta (Karachi): Nos 843, 844, 845.

Rangoon Dockyard: contracts transferred to Calcutta.

Shipbuilding Ltd (Auckland): Nos 407, 408, 409.

Star Shipyard (New Westminster): Nos 070, 071, 125, 126, 127.

Singapore Harbour Board: Nos 310, 311, 432, 433.

Taikoo Dock (Hong Kong): Nos 376, 377, 434, 435.

Task Rly & Port Service (Dar-es-Salaam): Nos 366, 367, 833, 834.

J.J. Taylor (Toronto): Nos 052, 053, 079, 080, 086, 088, 089, 090, 091, 112, 113.

Vancouver Shipyard: Nos 066, 067, 122, 123, 124.

Voss Ltd

    (Auckland): Nos 410, 411.

    (Singapore): Nos 362,363, 364, 365, 372, 373, 374, 375, 388, 389.

    (Alexandria): Nos 348, 349, 350, 351, 352, 353, 354, 355, 356, 357, 358, 359, 837, 838, 389, 840, 841, 842, 860, 861, 862, 863, 864, 865, 866, 866, 867, 868, 869, 870, 871, 872.

    (Bombay): Nos 390, 391, 420, 421.

    (Calcutta): Nos 416, 417, 419, 436 & 437 (both ex-Rangoon).

    (East London): Nos 848, 849, 850, 851, 856, 857.

    (Knysna): Nos 852, 853.

    (East Africa): Nos 4001, 4002, 4003, 4004,

Norman Wright (Brisbane): Nos 815, 816, 826.

Builders unknown: Nos 380, 381, 382, 392, 393, 394, 395, 396, 397, 398, 399, 442, 828, 873, 874, 875, 876, 877, 878, 879, 880, 881, 882, 883, 884, 885, 886, 887, 888, 889, 890, 891, 892, 893, 894, 895, 896, 897, 898, 899, 900.

Fairmile 'C' Type Motor Launches as Motor Gun Boats

HM ML	Completed	Builder
312	1941	Woodnutt (St Helens)
313	1941	Jas. Miller (St Monace)
314	1941	Dickie (Bangor)
315	1941	Alex-Robertson(Sandbank)
316	1941	Tough Bros (Teddington)
317	1941	Alex-Robertson (Sandbank)
318	1941	Aldous Successors (Brightlingsea)
319	1941	Brooke Marine (Lowestoft)
320	1941	Wm Osborne (Littlehampton)
321	1941	Jas. Silver (Rosneath)
322	1941	Dickie (Bangor)
323	1941	Kris Cruisers (Isleworth)
324	1941	Woodnutt (St Helens)
325	1941	Curtis (Looe)
326	1941	Jas. Silver (Rosneath)
327	1941	Builder unknown
328	1941	Lady Bee (Southwick)
329	1941	Aldou Successors (Brightlingsea)
330	1941	Tough Bros (Teddington)
331	1941	Tough Bros (Teddington)
332	1941	Jas. Silver (Rosneath)
333	1941	Woodnutt (St Helens)
334	1941	Dickie (Bangor)
335	1941	Dickie (Bangor)

Specification

Displacement tons	72
Dimensions	110 x 17½ x 5/6½
Armament	Two 2pdr, four .5in mg, four .303in mg
Machinery	Three shaft petrol engines, 2,700bhp
Speed	26½/23½ knots
Complement	16

Note: Built as an early gun boat derived from the Fairmile 'B' Type and with supercharged engines, but in appearance closer to the Fairmile 'A' Type.

Losses: HM ML313 was mined off Normandy on 16 August 1944, likewise ML326 on 26 June 1944.

HM ML314 was damaged by batteries at St Nazaire on 28 March 1942 and later sank.

HM ML328 sank after a surface action in the Dover Straits on 21 July 1942.

HM ML335 sank after a surface action in the North Sea on 10 September 1942.

ML316.
(Imperial War
Museum)

'C' Type
Fairmile.
(Imperial War
Museum)

Fairmile 'D' Type Motor Gun Boats, Motor Torpedo Boats, Interchangeable.

All built 1942–1944
Motor Gun Boats and Motor Torpedo Boats interchangeable and described in this text as
    MTB except as otherwise stated; MTBs 601–800.

Specification	MGB	MTB	MGB/MTB
Displacement tons	90	95	105
Dimensions	All craft 110wl, 115 x 21¼ x 5		
Armament	All craft one 2pdr, two 20mm, four .5in mg, four .303in mg		
Torpedo tubes		Two 21in	Four 18in
Depth Charges	2 plus	2 plus	2 plus
Machinery	All craft four shaft petrol engines, 5,000bhp		
Speed	31/27½ knots	31/27½ knots	29/26 knots
Complement	24	24	30

Note: Designed for two roles and the hardest hitting of all RN coastal craft. Some hulls built with scallops on the bow for the better clearance of torpedoes when discharged. Minelayers were in general of the Fairmile Modified 'P' Type but included boats 725 to 800 above.

Losses: HM MTB601 caught fire at Dover on 4 July 1942.

HM MTB605 foundered when off Ostend on 17 April 1945.

HM MTB606 sank after surface action off the Dutch coast on 14 November 1943.

HM MTB622 sank after surface action from German light forces near Terschelling on 10 March 1943.

HM MTB625 was lost in home waters in 1944, no other particulars available.

HM MTB626 caught fire at Lerwick on 22 November 1943.

HM MTB631 went aground on the Norwegian coast and was captured by German land forces on 14 March 1943.

HM MTB635 was damaged and expended as a target off Malta in July 1945.

HM MTB636 sank as a result of gunfire from enembatteries on Elba on 15 October 1943.

HM MTB639 sank after surface action with the Italian TB *Sagittario* when off Tunisia on 28 April 1943.

HM MTB640 was mined on 27 June 1944 when off Spezia.

HM MGB641 sank after severe gunfire from enemy batteries in the Straits of Messina on 14 July 1943.

HM MGB644 was mined west of Sicily on 26 June 1943 and sunk by own forces.

HM MGB648 sank after air attack when off Pantellaria on 14 June 1943.

HM MGB655 was mined in the Adriatic on 22 March 1945.

HM MGB657 was mined off Rimini on 12 February 1944.

HM MGB663 was mined off Rimini on 10 October 1944.

HM MGB665 sank from gunfire of shore batteries when off Messina 15 August 1943.

HM MTB666 sank after surface action against Dutch coast on 5 July 1944.

HM MTB669 sank after surface action against Norwegian coast on 26 October 1943.

HM MGB671 sank after surface action with German destroyers on 21 April 1944 when off Cape Barfleur.

HM MTB672 was mined on 29 April 1944.

HM MTB681 sank after surface action with German light forces off the Dutch coast on 10 June 1944.

HM MTB686 caught fire at Lerwick on 22 November 1943.

HM MTB690 sank after colliding with a wreck off Lowestoft on 18 January 1945.

HM MTB697 was mined in the Adriatic on 17 April 1945.

HM MTB705 was mined in the Adriatic on 23 March 1945.

HM MGB707 sank after colliding with the FFS *L'Escarmouche* off the coast of Ulster, on 18 August 1944.

HM MGB708 was attacked in error by Allied aircraft in the English Channel and finally sunk by own forces on 5 May 1944.

HM MTB710 was mined on 10 April 1945 when off Zara.

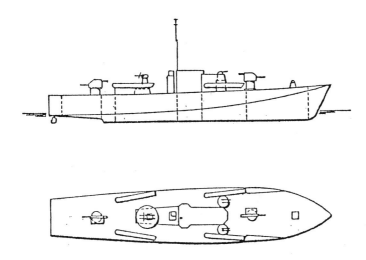

'D' Type Fairmile 1942.

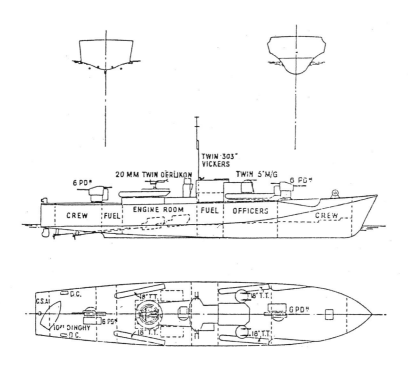

Outline of 'D' Type MTB.

'D' Type Fairmile. (Wright & Logan)

HM MTB712 was lost off Scapa and formally paid off on 19 July 1945.

HM MTB715 sank after an explosion at Fosnavaag on 19 May 1945.

HM MTB732 was attacked in error by FFS *La Combattante* on 28 May 1944 in the English Channel.

HM MTB734 was attacked in error by an allied aircraft on 26 June 1944 but the still floating hull was sunk by units of the Royal Navy in the North Sea.

HM MTBs 776, 789, 791 and 798 were lost in the Port of Ostend as a result of an explosion and later, fire, due to unsafe ordnance on 12 February 1945.

HM MTB782 was mined in the estuary of the Scheldt on 19 December 1944.

Builder	
Austin's (East Ham)	745, 773, 798.
Boat Construction Co. (Falmouth)	635, 650, 659.
Brooke Marine (Lowestoft)	611, 622, 639, 660, 681, 695, 711, 729, 762.
Collins (Lowestoft)	740, 783.
Dickie (Bangor)	604, 620, 638, 647, 671, 679, 714, 717, 717, 726, 750, 771, 777.
Dickie (Tarbert)	615, 629, 664.
Dorset Yacht (Hamsworthy)	619, 624, 633, 648, 662, 666, 685, 699, 713, 732, 752, 778, 800.
J. Hall (Glampton)	612, 613, 645, 652, 702.
P.K. Harris (Appledore)	618, 627, 642, 665, 687, 723, 757, 788.
Wm King (Burnham-on-Crouch)	609, 631, 667.
Kris Cruisers (Isleworth)	602, 632, 666.
Lady Bee (Southwick)	654.
Wm Osborne (Littleharnpton)	605, 616, 617, 634, 655, 663, 700, 710, 728, 748, 749, 787, 795.
Risdon Beazley (Northam)	646, 649.
Leo A. Robinson (Lowestoft)	770.

Alex–Robertson (Sandbank)	625, 630, 637, 653, 661, 675, 691, 781, 731, 758.
Jas. A. Silver (Rosneath)	607, 608, 621, 636.
Sussex-Shipbuilding (Shoreham)	774.
Thomson & Balfour (Bo'ness)	641, 668.
Tough Bros (Teddington)	601, 603, 626, 644, 651, 673, 674, 703.
J.W.&A. Upham (Brixham)	628, 658.
Wallasea Bay Yacht Stn	606, 623, 640, 658.
Woodnutt (St Helens)	610, 614, 643, 657, 684, 697, 715, 730, 759, 799.
Builders Unknown	669, 670, 672, 676, 678, 680, 682, 683, 686, 688, 690, 692, 694, 696, 698, 701, 704, 709, 712, 716, 719, 722, 724, 725, 717, 733, 739, 741, 744, 746, 751, 753, 756, 760, 761, 763, 769, 772, 775, 776, 779, 782, 784, 786, 794, 797.

Modified Fairmile 'D' Type, Interchangeable Motor Gun Boats/ Motor Torpedo Boats

HM MGB/MTB	Completed	Builder
5001	1944	Woodnutt (St Helens)
5002	1944	Not known
5003	1944	Not known
5004	1944	Not known
5005	1944	Wm Osborne (Littlehampton)
5006	1944	Not known
5007	1944	Not known
5008	1944	Not known
5009	1944	Not known
5010	1944	Dickie (Bangor)
5011	1944	Not known
5012	1944	Austins (East Ham)
5013	1944	Austins (East Ham)
5014	1944	Woodnutt (St Helens)
5015	1944	Not known
5016	1944	Not known
5017	1944	Not known
5018	1944	Not known
5019	1944	Not known
5020	1944	Wm Osborne (Littlehampton)
5021	1944	Not known
5022 (ex-75)	1944	Brooke Marine (Lowestoft)
5024	1944	Dickie (Bangor)
5025	1944	Not known
5026	1944	Not known

5027	1944	Not known
5028	1944	Woodnutt (St Helens)
5029	1944	Not known

Specification

Displacement tons	As for Fairmile 'D' Type
Dimensions	110wl.115 x 21¼ x 5
Armament	Two 6pdr and two 20mm
Torpedo tubes	Two 21in
Machinery	Four shaft petrol engines, 5,000bhp
Speed	As for Fairmile 'D' Type
Complement	As for Fairmile 'D' Type

Note: Some of this type were completed as Long Range Rescue Craft for the RAF.
Loss: HM MGB5001 sank after a surface action with an E-boat on 7 April 1945.

Fairmile 'F' Type Motor Gun Boat

This was a one ship class of which very little is known except that she was named HM
MGB2001 and had a displacement tonnage of 101.

Specification

Machinery	Four shaft petrol engines, 7,000bhp
Speed	36 knots
Builder	Kris Cruisers (Isleworth) in 1943

Modified 'D' type Fairmile. (Wright & Logan)

Chapter 15

Fairmile Harbour Defence Motor Launches

Fairmile Harbour Defence Motor Launch (HDML)

With the advent and success of the Second World War Coastal Forces, the need for a smaller, but equally seaworthy craft was quickly realised. Consequently, the Harbour Defence Motor Launch (just slightly smaller than the MLs of the First World War) was designed and rapidly built.

Harbour Defence Motor Launches 1001–1600 all built 1940–1944

Specification

Displacement tons	46
Dimensions	72 x 15 x 4½
Armament	One 2pdr, two twin .303in mg, one Holman Projector for flares
Anti-submarine	Eight depth charges were normally carried
Minesweeping	HDMLs landed their depth charges when fitted with the Oropesa minesweeping gear
Fuel	1,500 gallons diesel fuel with an additional 200 gallon deck tanks
Complement	10
Machinery	Two diesel engines of 150hp each plus an auxiliary lighting set. The two propellers gave 11/12 knots maximum
Range	1,000nm at 12 knots, 2,000 at 10 knots

Construction note: Variations in Australian-built HDMLs:

Displacement	58
Dimensions	80¼ x 16¼ x 9¼
Armament (Designed)	One 2pdr, two .303in Lewis mg, two .303in Stripped Lewis mg, ten depth charges
Armament (Actual)	Two 20mm DP, two single mtd .303in Vickers, eight depth charges
Machinery	Two diesel engines of 390bhp to two shafts
Complement	12
Range	3,000nm at 9 knots
Speed	As other HDMLs

Losses: HM HDML1003 was lost on 20 April 1941 when in transit across the North Atlantic.

HM HDML1011 while off Crete, was bombed by German aircraft on 10 May 1941.

HM HDML1015 was wrecked off Alexandria Harbour in October 1943.

HM HDML1019 became a constructive total loss after a fire at Freetown in July 1944.

HM HDML1030 was lost, cause unknown, north of Alexandria on 28 May 1941. Later raised and deployed post-war in the Malayan Emergency.

HM HDML1039 was lost at Tobruk but cause unknown on 23 June 1942.

HM HDML1054 was wrecked off West Hartlepool on 23 October 1943.

HM HDML1057 when off Killindini was mined on 13 October 1944.

HM HDML1060 was lost in an explosion at Poole Harbour on 7 August 1944.

HM HDML1062 was engaged by Japanese surface craft in Banka Straits on the 16 February 1942.

HM HDML1063 was engaged by Japanese surface craft off Tan Jong Priok on 1 March 1942.

HM HDML1069 was mined in Tobruk Harbour on 23 June 1942.

HM HDML1083 whilst transiting the Gulf of Kos foundered in bad weather, on 20 February 1944.

HM HDML1100 and 1101 foundered in the Naaf River, in April 1942.

HM HDML1119 took the ground off Ceylon on 7 October 1944.

HM HDML1121 in bad weather foundered off Pantellaria on 31 December 1943.

HM HDML1147 was lost by fire in Freetown Harbour in July 1944.

HM HDML1154 was mined at Bizerta on 14 May 1943.

HM HDML1163 was torpedoed in the Western Approaches by a German surface vessel on 5 January 1945.

HM HDML1179 foundered north of Jamaica in bad weather on 21 August 1944.

HM HDML1226 was mined off Alexandropolis on 4 October 1945.

HM HDML1227 was attacked by German surface craft on 5 October 1944 when off Piraeus.

HM MDML1259 came under shellfire from German shore batteries off Marseilles on 31 October 1944.

HM HDML1380 foundered in the Aegean Sea in bad weather on 1 May 1944.

HM HDML1381 was taken by German forces at Sirina on 26 August 1944.

HM HDML1388 went ashore and was wrecked off West Hartlepool on 24 December 1943.

HM HDML1417 was mined off Flushing on 15 February 1945.

HM HDML1037 was lost in transit on 20 April 1941 as HDML1003.

HM HDML1090 was lost in transit from the UK on 11 July 1942.

HM HDML1153 was lost in transit from the UK in September 1942.

HM HDMLs 1157 and 1212 were both lost in transit from the UK in April 1943.

HM HDMLs 1244 and 1289 were both lost in transit from the UK on 11 November 1943.

HM HDMLs 1092, 1093, 1094 and 1095 were destroyed while fitting out at Belfast in 1941, due to a German air attack.

HDMLs 1102, 1103 and 1104 were destroyed incomplete by own forces at Rangoon in April 1942 in the face of the Japanese advance.

HDMLs 1096, 1167, 1168, 1169 and 1170 were lost on the stocks at Singapore in February 1942 in the face of the Japanese advance.

HDML1024. (Imperial War Museum)

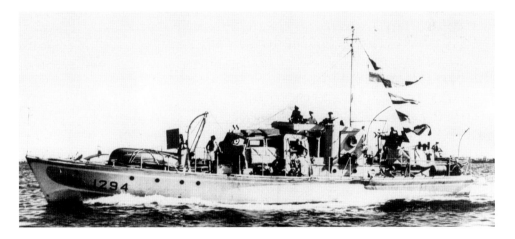

HDML1294. (Imperial War Museum)

Additional loss: HM HDML1323, whilst on patrol in the Pearl River to the west of the colony of Hong Kong, on 9 September 1953, halted a junk for search purposes. A Chinese Landing Craft of the Peoples Liberation Army (Navy) approached from Canton requesting that HM ship stop. This was not complied with and both vessels neared each other. The Chinese Landing Craft opened fire, causing fatalities on the Royal Navy HDML, which became a constructive total loss.

Overseas construction note: HDMLs built in Australia were of different dimensions from those built in UK boat yards, these being 80¼ x 16¼ x 9¼ (deep). Those built in US yards were offered under Lease Lend and, as none were lost in Commonwealth service, were returned after the conclusion of the Second World War.

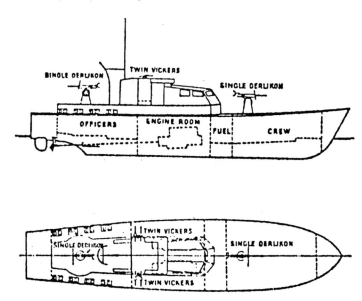

Outline of HDML 72ft.

Builders (HDMLs built in the UK)

Anderson, Rigden &Perkins (Whitstable): Nos 1009, 1010, 1146, 1147, 1233, 1234, 1273, 1274, 1275, 1382, 1383, 1403, 1404, 1479, 1480.

Berthon Boat (Lymington): Nos 1013, 1014, 1025, 1026, 1031, 1032, 1037, 1038, 1046, 1047, 1125–1128, 1237–1240, 1255–1260, 1372, 1373, 1390–1393, 1413, 1414, 1465–1468, 1483.

Wm. Blackmore (Bideford): Nos 1015, 1016, 1065, 1066, 1083, 1084, 1150–1153, 1231, 1232, 1300–1303.

Graham Bunn (Wroxham): Nos 1019, 1020, 1036, 1054, 1055, 1154, 1155, 1308, 1309, 1310.

Bute Slip Lock (Port Bannatyne): Nos 1156, 1157, 1279, 1280.

E.F. Eilkins (Christchurch): Nos 1080, 1162–1166, 1398, 1399.

Harland & Wolff (Belfast): Nos 1017, 1018, 1034, 1035, 1092–1095.

D. Hilyard (Littlehampton): Nos 1005, 1006, 1044, 1056, 1057, 1158, 1159, 1235, 1236, 1269–1272, 1401.

Lady Bee (Southwick): Nos 1001, 1002.

McGruer (Clynder): Nos 1029, 1030, 1048–1050, 1229, 1230, 1296–1299, 1380, 1381.

McLean (Renfrew): Nos 1076–1079, 1241–1244, 1394, 1395, 1407, 1408, 1476, 1477, 1478.

A. H. Moody (Swannick Shore): Nos 1148, 1149, 1221, 1222, 1276, 1277, 1278,.

Morgan Giles (Teignmouth): Nos 1039, 1051, 1052, 1053.

Alfred Mylne (Port Bannatyne): Nos 1027, 1028.

R. A. Newman (Hamworthy): Nos 1011, 1012, 1040–1043, 1225, 1226, 1384, 1385, 1386, 1387, 1590.

Leo Robinson   (Lowestoft): Nos 1021, 1022, 1075, 1137, 1138, 1247, 1248, 1396, 1397
                (Tewkesbury): Nos 1073, 1074, 1139, 1245, 1246.

Sittingbourne Sbdg.: Nos 1023, 1024, 1071, 1072, 1160, 1161, 1227, 1228, 1281, 1282, 1388, 1389.

Sussex Sbdg. (Shoreham): Nos 1023, 1024, 1292, 1293, 1294, 1295.

Thornycroft (Hampton): Nos 1129–1136, 1211, 1212, 1283–1291.

Watercraft (East Molesey): Nos 1003, 1004, 1069, 1070.

Herbert Woods (Potter Heigham): Nos 1142–1145, 1304–1307.

(Shoreham): Nos 1007, 1008, 1085–1087, 1211–1214.

(Poole): Nos 1033, 1045, 1064, 1081, 1082, 1140, 1141, 1209, 1210, 1249–1254.

(Yarmouth): Nos 1058, 1059, 1060, 1061.

(Southampton): Nos 1067, 1068.

(Dumbarton): Nos 1088, 1089.

(Isle of Wight): Nos 1090, 1091.

Builders unknown: Nos 1400–1402, 1405, 1406, 1461, 1462, 1469, 1484, 1485, 1501–1589, 1591–1600.

Builders (HDMLs built abroad)

Ackerman Boat Works (Azusa): Nos 1348, 1349, 1350, 1351.

African Marine & General Eng. (Mombasa): Nos 1105–1108, 1195, 1196.

Dodge Boat Works (Newport News): Nos 1171–1182, 1364–1367.

Elscot Boats (City Island): Nos 1356, 1357, 1358, 1359.

Everett Marine Rly. (Washington): Nos 1187, 1188, 1189, 1190.

Freeport Port Shipyard (Long Island): Nos 1352, 1353, 1354, 1355.

Garden Reach (Calcutta): Nos 1115, 1120.

Grays Hbr. Shpg. (Aberdeen): Nos 1191, 1192, 1193, 1194.

Hooghly Dock & Eng. (Calcutta): Nos 1112, 1113.

Irrawadi Flotilla Co. (Rangoon): Nos 1100, 1101, 1102, 1103.

E. Jack (Launceston): Nos 1325, 1326, 1329.

Wm. Edgar John (Rye): Nos 1360, 1361, 1362, 1363.

Chas. P. Leek (New Jersey): Nos 1338, 1339.

MacFarlane (Adelaide): Nos 1323, 1324, 1328.

Madden & Lewis (Sausalito): Nos 1183, 1184, 1185, 1186.

H. Mohatta (Karachi): Nos 1109, 1110, 1111, 1265, 1266, 1267.

Frederick Nichol (Durban): Nos 1098, 1099, 1197–1202, 1330–1337.

Pehara Land Co. (Alexandria): Nos 1315–1320.

Purdon & Featherstone (Hobart): Nos 1321, 1322, 1327.

Rangoon Dockyard: No.1104.

Spradbrow (Durban): Nos 1203, 1204.

L. S. Thorsen (Ellesworth): Nos 1340, 1341, 1342, 1343.

Truscott Boat & Dock Co. (St Joseph): Nos 1348, 1349, 1350, 1351.

Walker, Son & Co.   (Colombo): Nos 1205, 1206, 1207, 1208.

(Singapore): Nos 1062, 1063, 1096, 1097.

(Calcutta): Nos 1118, 1119.

(Bombay): Nos 1114, 1116, 1117, 1261–1264, 1268.

(Ceylon): Nos 1311, 1312, 1313, 1314.

Builders unknown: Nos 1167–1170, 1213–1220, 1409–1412, 1415–1460, 1463, 1464, 1470–1475, 1481, 1482, 1486–1500.

Chapter 16

Landing Craft Support

Landing Barge Flak

Initials LB(F) No.1 and others
These were swim barges requisitioned by the Admiralty for many tasks and were powered
by twin petrol engines, 300bhp.

Specification
Speed   7 knots
Armament   Two 40mm on Army wheeled mountings, plus two 20mm or four .303in mg
Complement 6
Troops   16 approximately

Note: The LB(F)s were conceived due to the shortage of the smaller Landing Craft, and
carried two Army Bofors guns which could be fired from the barge. When the barge
grounded on the beach, the Bofors were discharged down the newly modified ramped
stern to join the appropriate Army detachment on shore. The troops that embarked
with the guns fought with their guns both at sea and, more normally, on shore.
Losses: Not known.

Landing Barge Gun

Initials   LB(G) No.1 and others
These swim barges were requisitioned as mentioned above for the LB(F).

Specification
Speed   7 knots
Armament   Two 25pdr on Army mountings, two 20mm
Complement 6
Troops   16 approximately

Note: As for LB(F) (see above).
Losses: Not known.

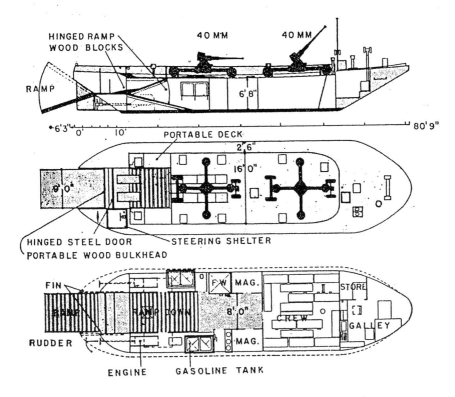

Landing Barge Flack LB(F).

Landing Craft Support Medium Mark I

Initials   LCS(M)(I)
War-built Nos 1–24

Specification

Displacement tons	9/10½
Dimensions	41½ x 10 x 2
Armament	One 4in smoke mortar, two .5in mg
Machinery	Two shaft petrol engines, 130bhp
Speed	10 knots
Complement	11

Note: When Landing Craft were first conceived it was apparent that, as they were of such shallow draught, no ship of the Fleet would be able to escort them once they had left the protection of the Landing Fleet. In consequence, a percentage of all types of Landing Craft were fitted with additional weapons proportionate to their size to defend and protect the other Landing Craft which were carrying troops, vehicles, artillery and armoured vehicles.

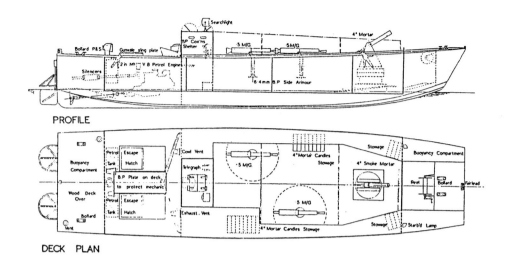

PROFILE

DECK PLAN

LCS(M)I, Landing Craft Support Medium Mk1.

Losses: HM LCS (M)(1) lost in 1941, date place and cause unknown.
HM LCS4 was lost on 20 June 1942 at Tobruk.
HM LCS6 was lost on 20 June 1942 at Tobruk.
HM LCS9 was lost on 19 August 1942 in Operation Jubilee (Dieppe).
HM LCS11 was lost in November 1942 during Operation Torch (North Africa).
HM LCS14 was lost in November 1942 during Operation Torch.
HM LCS15 was lost on 20 June 1942 at Tobruk.
HM LCS18 was lost on 20 June 1942 at Tobruk.
HM LCS19 was lost on 20 June 1942 at Tobruk.
HM LCS22 was lost on 20 June 1942 at Tobruk.
HM LCS16 was lost on 29 August 1943 in India.
HM LCS17 sank after an engagement with enemy forces on 25 April 1943 on the Mayu River, Burma.
HM LCS23 was lost while on patrol in the Mayu River, Burma, in March 1943.

Landing Craft Support Medium Mark 2

Initials LCS(M)(2)
War-built Nos 25–40

Specification
Displacement tons   10½/12½
Dimensions   41½ x 10 x 2
Armament   One 4in smoke mortar, two .5in mg

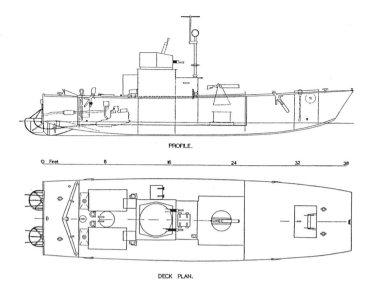

PROFILE.

O Feet 8 16 24 32 38

DECK PLAN.

LCS(M)II, Landing Craft Support Medium Mk2.

LCS(M)33. (Imperial War Museum)

Machinery	Two shaft petrol engines, 130bhp
Speed	10 knots
Complement	11

Losses: HM LCS(M)(2)28 was lost in November 1942 during Operation Torch (North Africa).

HM LCS30 was lost during operations off the Arakan Coast in June 1945.

Landing Craft Support Medium Mark 3

Initials LCS(M)(3)	
Built 1943–1943, Nos 41–120	
Displacement tons	11½/13¼
Dimensions	41¾ x 10 x 2
Armament	One 4in smoke mortar, two .5in mg, two .303in mg
Machinery	Two shaft petrol engines, 130bhp
Speed	10 knots
Complement	11

Losses: HM LCS(M)(3)42 was lost on 25 August 1945, cause and place unknown.

HM LCS46 was lost in Operation Shingle (Anzio) in January 1944.

HM LCS47 was lost in 1944, cause and place unknown.

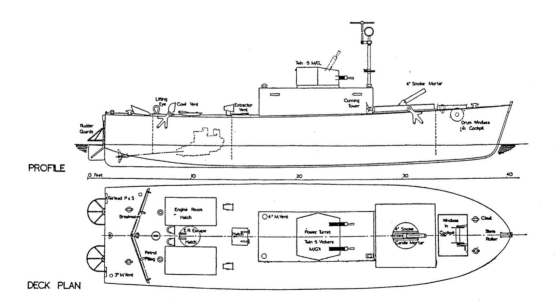

LCS(M)III, Landing Craft Support Medium Mk3.

LCS(M)47. (Imperial War Museum)

HM LCS49 was lost on 25 August 1945, cause and place unknown.

HM LCS54 was lost on 1 July 1944, cause and place unknown.

HM LCS59 was lost during May 1944, cause and place unknown.

HM LCS69 was lost on 3 March 1944 off East Scotland during exercises.

HM LCS75 was lost in June 1944 during Operation Neptune (Normandy).

HM LCS76 was lost in June 1944 during Operation Neptune.

HM LCS80 was lost in June 1944 during Operation Neptune.

HM LCS81 was lost in June 1944 during Operation Neptune.

HM LCS83 was lost in June 1944 during Operation Neptune.

HM LCS91 was lost in June 1944 during Operation Neptune.

HM LCS99 was lost in June 1944 during Operation Neptune.

HM LCS101 was lost in June 1944 during Operation Neptune.

HM LCS103 was lost in June 1944 during Operation Neptune.

HM LCS108 was lost in June 1944 during Operation Neptune.

HM LCS114 was lost in June 1944 during Operation Neptune.

HM LCS148 was lost off the Arakan coast in June 1945.

Landing Craft Support Large Mark 1

Initials LCS(L)(1)
Built 1943–1944 Nos 1–250

Specification

Displacement tons	20/24½
Dimensions	47 x 12½ x 2/4
Armament	One 4in smoke mortar, one 2pdr, two .5in mg, two .303in mg
Machinery	Twin diesel engines, 330bhp
Speed	10¾ knots
Complement	13

Loss: HM LCS(1)201 was lost in September 1943 in a collision in the English Channel.

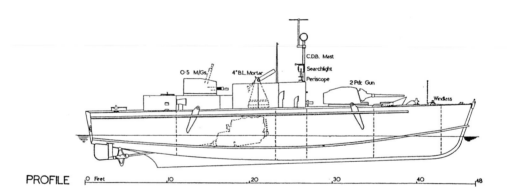

LCS(L)I, Landing Craft Support Large Mk1.

LCS(L)1. (Imperial War Museum)

Landing Craft Support Large Mark 2

Initials LCS(L)(2)
War built Nos 251–260

Specification

Displacement tons	84/112
Dimensions	105 x 21½ x 2¼/3¼
Armament	One 4in smoke mortar, one 6pdr, two 20mm, two .5in mg
Machinery	Two shaft petrol engines, 1,140bhp
Speed	14½ knots
Complement	25

Note: Also known as the Fairmile 'H' Type.
Losses: HM LCS(L)(2)252 was lost on 1 November 1944 during Operation Infatuate (Walcheren).
HM LCS256 was lost on 1 November 1944 during Operation Infatuate.
HM LCS258 was lost on 1 November 1944 during Operation Infatuate.

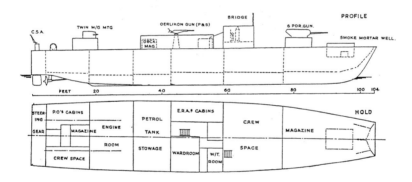

LCS(L)II, Landing Craft Support Large Mk2.

LCS(L)256. (Imperial War Museum)

Landing Craft Flak Mark 2, later LCF(L)

Initials LCF(2)
War-built Nos 1 and 2

Specification

Displacement tons	539
Dimensions	160 x 31 x 3¾/7
Armament	Four 4in DP AA, three 20mm for LCF(2)1
	Eight 2pdr, four 20mm AA for LCF(2)2
Machinery	Three shaft diesel engines, 1,380bhp
Speed	11 knots
Complement	LCF(2)1 74
	LCF(2)2 67

Losses: HM LCF(2)1 blew up and sank on 17 August 1944 during Operation Neptune
(Normandy).
HM LCF2 was lost on 19 August 1942 during Operation Jubilee (Dieppe).

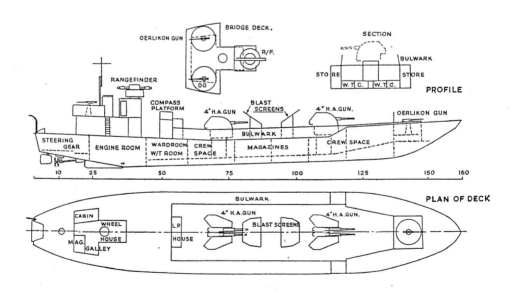

Landing Craft Flak Mk2.

Landing Craft Flak Mark 3, later LCF(L)

Initials LCF(3)
War-built Nos 3–6 Group 1, 7–18 Group 2

Displacement tons	470
Dimensions	190¾ x 31 x 3¾/7
Armament	Group 1 Eight 2pdr, four 20mm all AA
	Group 2 Four 2pdr, eight 20mm all AA
Machinery	Two shaft diesel engines, 920bhp
Speed	11 knots
Complement	Group 1 62
	Group 2 66

Losses: HM LCF(3)13 was lost after an enemy aircraft attack when off Pantellaria on 12 June 1943.
HM LCF18 was mined, while in convoy during Operation Brassard (Elba).

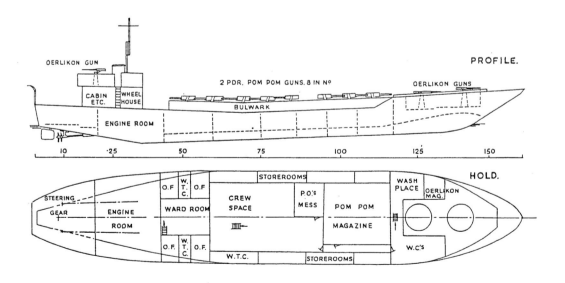

Landing Craft Flak Mk3.

Landing Craft Flak Mark 4, later LCF(L)

Initials LCF(4)
War-built Nos 19–46

Specification

Displacement tons	415
Dimensions	187¼ x 38¾ x 3½/4½
Armament	Four 2pdr, eight 20mm
Machinery	Two shaft diesel engines, 920bhp
Speed	11 knots
Complement	66

Losses: HM LCF(4)31 was lost in September 1944 during Operation Neptune (Normandy).
HM LCF37 was lost on 1 November 1944 during Operation Infatuate (Walcheren).
HM LCF38 was lost on 1 November 1944 during Operation Infatuate.

Landing Craft Gun Large Mark 3

Initials LCG(L)(3)
War-built Nos 1–30

Specification

Displacement tons	491
Dimensions	190¾ x 31 x 3¾/7
Armament	Two 4.7in, three to five 20mm
Machinery	Two shaft diesel engines, 920bhp
Speed	10 knots
Complement	27

Note: The 4.7in guns were from badly damaged destroyers.
Losses: HM LCG(L)(3)1 was lost on 2 November 1944 during Operation Infatuate.
HM LCG2 was lost on 2 November 1944 during Operation Infatuate.
HM LCG15 was lost in heavy weather off Milford Haven on 25 April 1943.
HM LCG16 was lost in heavy weather off Milford Haven on 26 April 1943.

Opposite top: LC(F)24. (Imperial War Museum)

Opposite middle: LCG(L)(3)2. (Imperial War Museum)

Opposite bottom: Landing Craft Gun Large Mk3.

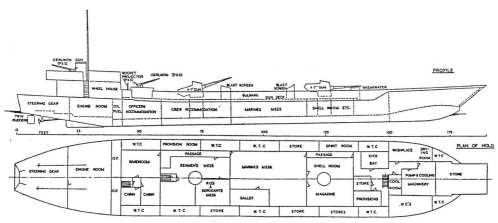

Landing Craft Gun Large Mark 4

Initials LCG(L)(4)
War-built Nos 680, 681, 687, 764, 831, 939, 1007, 1062, and others

Specification

Displacement tons	570
Dimensions	185½ x 38¾ x 3¾/4½
Armament	Two 4.7in, ten to fourteen 20mm
Machinery	Two shaft diesel engines, 920bhp
Speed	10 knots
Complement	48

Losses: HM LCG(L)(4)764 was lost during Operation Neptune (Normandy) in the period July to August 1944.

HM LCG831 was lost during Operation Neptune in the period July to August 1944.

HM LCG1062 was lost during Operation Neptune in the period July to August 1944.

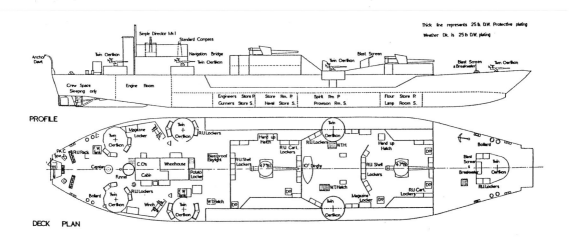

Landing Craft Gun Large Mk4.

Opposite above: Landing Craft Gun, Medium Mk1.

Opposite below: LCG(L)(1)101. (Imperial War Museum)

Landing Craft Gun Medium Mark 1

Initials LCG(M)(1)
Built 1944 Nos 101–200

Specification

Displacement tons	270/381
Dimensions	154¼ x 22¼ x 6
Armament	Two 17pdr or two 25pdr, two 20mm AA
Machinery	Two shaft diesel engines, 920/1,000bhp
Speed	13½/11¾ knots
Complement	31/35

Losses: HM LCG(M)(1)101 was lost on 1 November 1944 during Operation Infatuate (Walcheren).
HM LCG102 was lost on 1 November 1944 during Operation Infatuate.

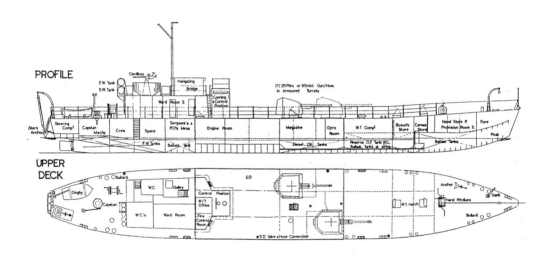

Landing Craft Support Rocket

Initials LCT(R) Nos 334, 425, 452, 457, 460, 473, 1064, 1405 and others
All converted from Landing Craft Tank Mark II and Landing Craft Tank Mark III and
retained their original numbers.

Specification	LCT(2) hull	LCT(3) hull
Displacement tons	296/453	350/640 or 625
Dimensions	160 x 31 x 3¾/7	190¾ x 31 x 3¾/7
Armament	795 5in rockets	1080 5in rockets
	Two 2pdr or two 20mm	Two 2pdr or two 20mm
Machinery	Three shaft petrol engines or diesel engines	
Speed	10½ or 11 knots	10½ or 11 knots
Complement	60 plus	60 plus

Note: The discharge of a full salvo of 5in rockets would normally saturate an area of
coast/beach of about 800 x 200 square yards. The reload of the second salvo took over
three hours. The discharge normally took place when the LCS(R) was 1¾ nm off shore
from the intended target.

Loss: HM LCT(R)457 was mined off Ostend on 5 November 1944.

LCT(R)334. (Imperial War Museum)

Landing Craft Support were always in short supply and losses were quite heavy. A type designated for South East Asia and the Pacific areas was planned and would have been built from LCG(M)(1) hulls to evolve as the LCG(2) but none entered service. Similarly the LCT(R)s were to have been increased in numbers by the more seaworthy LCS(R) of which thirty would have been commissioned but only one – LCS(R) – entered service before the end of hostilities. The Second World War saw the loss of 1,308 Landing Ships, Craft and Barges.

Description of Landing Craft was helped by the mark number of certain types but certain authorities give both Roman and Arabic numbers for the same craft in the same document, e.g. LCG(L)(III) and LCG(L)(3) are the same type. In this section on Landing Craft Support, the latter number group has largely been given.

Builders

Sir William Arrol (Meadowside)	LCF(3)15, 16, LCG(L)(3)1, LCT(R)460, 473, LCG(M)(1)143–150, LCG(M)(2)513–524 and eight more.
Austin's (East Ham)	LCS(L)(2)251.
Berthon Boat (Lymington)	LCS(M)(1)23, 24.
Brooke Marine (Lowestoft)	LCS(L)(2)255.
Denny (Dumbarton)	LCG(L)(4)687.
Dickie (Bangor)	LCS(L)(2)254.
Alex-Finlay (Motherwell)	LCF(4)19 plus two more, fifteen LCG(L), four LCT(R).
Fleming & Ferguson (Paisley)	LCG(L)(3)26.
General Steam Navigation Co. (Deptford)	LCG(M)120, 187, LCF(3)9, 10.
H.T. Percival (Horning)	LCS(L)253, 259.
Jas. Pollock (Faversham)	LCF(3)11.

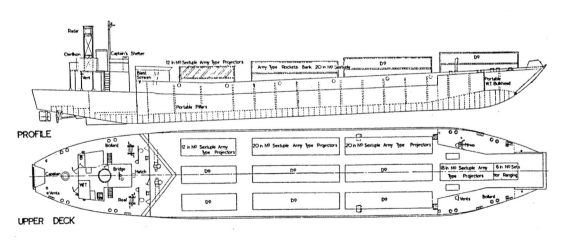

Landing Craft Support Rocket Mk3.

Redpath Brown (Meadowside)	LCF(3)17, 18.
J. Russell (London)	LCF(3)7, 8.
Solent Shipyard (Sarisbury Green)	LCS(L)252, 258.
Stockton Construction Co.	LCG(M)(1)175–190, LCF(3)13, 14, LCF(4)35, LCG(L)(3)3, LCS(R)25–29.
Tees Side Bridge & Eng. (Middlesbrough)	LCF(3)1, 2 (both completed Palmers Hebburn), 3, LCF(4)38, LCG(L)3, 2, LCG(M)(1)124, 127, LCS(R)5, 10.
Thornycroft (Woolston)	Twenty-four LCS(M).
Tilbury Dredging & Contracting (Greenwich)	LCF(3)12.

Chapter 17

Interchangeable Fast Patrol Craft

Ex-German S-boats

HMS		Completed	Builder
FPB 5208	(ex-MTB5208) (ex-S208)	1942/44	Lurssen Vegesack
FPB5212	(ex-MTB5212) (ex-S212)	1942/44	Lurssen Vegesack

Specification (as built)

Displacement tons	92½
Dimensions	114¾– x 16¾ x 4¾
Armament	One 37mm, three 20mm all AA
Torpedo tubes	Two 21in and two reloads
Machinery	Three shaft diesel engines, 7,500/6,000bhp
Speed	41/38 knots
Range	700nm at 35 knots
Complement	21
Fuel	16¾ tons oil

MTB5212. (Source not known)

Note: These two S-boats (commonly known as E-boats) were recovered intact at the surrender of Germany in 1945 and, in 1955, were retained for experimental purposes at HMS *Hornet*, the Coastal Forces main base.

Ex-German R-boat

HM ML	Completed	Builder
6115 (ex-R 113)	1939/43	Abeking & Rasmussen (Lemwerder)

Specification (as built)

Displacement tons	125
Dimensions	124 x 19 x 4½
Armament	One 37mm AA, three to six 20mm
Machinery	Two shaft diesel engines, 1,800bhp
Speed	20 knots
Range	1,100nm at 15 knots
Complement	3
Fuel	10 tons oil

Note: This Motor Minesweeper was commissioned into the Royal Navy as a Motor Launch for evaluation of different naval tasks.

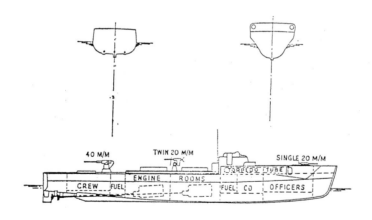

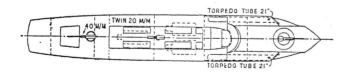

Outline of Schnell Boat (E-boat).

P6012 Class, Rhine Flotilla

HMS
HM ML6009
HM ML6010
HM ML6011
HM ML6012
HM ML6013
HM ML6014

Specification
Displacement tons   75
Dimensions   91 x 16¼ x 5¼
Armament   Three 20mm

Note: These six launches constituted the Royal Navy's Rhine Flotilla as at 1955.
Note of origin: All six craft are ex-German Air Sea Rescue launches.

ML6012. (Wright & Logan)

'Proud' Class Interchangeable MGB/MTB

HMS	Completed*	Builder
Proud Fusilier (ex-MTB505)		British Power Boat Co.
Proud Grenadier (ex-MTB506)		British Power Boat Co.
Proud Guardsman (ex-MTB507)		British Power Boat Co.
Proud Highlander (ex-MTB508)		British Power Boat Co.
Proud Knight (ex-MTB509)		British Power Boat Co.
Proud Lancer (ex-MTB519)		British Power Boat Co.
Proud Legionary (ex-MTB522)		British Power Boat Co.
Proud Patriot (ex-MTB596)		British Power Boat Co.
Proud Patroller (ex-MTB598)		British Power Boat Co.

Specification

Displacement tons	44
Dimensions	71¾ x 20½ x 5¾
Armament	One 6pdr, two 20mm, four mg in some
Torpedo tubes	Two 18in
Machinery	Three petrol engines, 4,050bhp
Speed	39 knots
Sea Speed	32 knots
Complement	17

Note: In 1955 *Proud Legionary* was unarmed except for the 18in torpedoes.
*See page 144 for wartime construction of these boats.

'Bold' Class Fast Patrol Boats

HMS	Completed	Builder
Bold Pathfinder (ex-MTB5720)	1953	Vosper Ltd
Bold Pioneer (ex-MTB5701)	1953	J.S. White & Co.

Specification	*Bold Pathfinder*	*Bold Pioneer*
Displacement tons	130	130
Dimensions	122¾ x 20¼ x 6½	121 x 25½ x 6¾
Armament (as MGB)	Two 4.5in, 25 cal, One 40mm Bofors	Two 4.5in, 25 cal. One 40mm Bofors
Armament (as MTB)	One 40mm Bofors and four 21in torpedo tubes	One 40mm Bofors and four 21in torpedo tubes
Machinery	Two G2 gas turbines 9,000shp and two diesels, 5,000bhp	Two G2 gas turbines 9,000shp and two diesels, 5,000bhp
Speed	40 knots approx.	40 knots approx.
Complement	20	18

Bold Pathfinder. (Vosper Thornycroft)

Note: HMS *Bold Pathfinder* was built as an experimental development of an MTB of light
alloy construction and twin funnels abreast. She had four screws and four rudders.
HMS *Bold Pioneer* was the second experimental twin gas turbine propelled
interchangeable MGB/MTB of timber construction, and was very similar in
appearance to *Bold Pathfinder.*

'Gay' Class Motor Torpedo Boats Interchangeable

HMS	Completed	Builder
Gay Archer	1952	Vosper Ltd
Gay Bombardier	1952	Vosper Ltd
Gay Bowman	1952	Vosper Ltd
Gay Bruiser	1952	Vosper Ltd
Gay Carabineer	1953	J.I. Thornycroft & Co.
Gay Cavalier	1953	J. Taylor
Gay Centurion	1952	J.I. Thornycroft & Co.
Gay Charger	1953	Morgan Giles Ltd
Gay Charioteer	1953	Morgan Giles Ltd
Gay Dragoon	1953	J. Taylor
Gay Fencer	1953	McGrue Boats Ltd
Gay Forester	1954	McGrue Boats Ltd

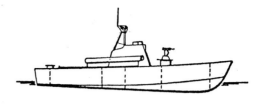

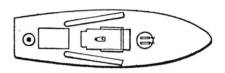

Right: 'Gay' Class 1953.

Below: Gay Bombardier. (Vosper Thornycroft)

Specification

Displacement tons	50
Dimensions	75¼ x 20 x 4½
Armament (as MGB)	One 4.5in, 25 cal, one 40mm Bofors
Armament (as MTB)	Two 40mm Bofors and two 21in torpedo tubes
Machinery	Two petrol engines, 5,000bhp
Speed	40 knots
Sea Speed	30/35 knots
Complement	13

Note: Built as interchangeable short MGB/MTBs of wood construction.

'Dark' Class Motor Torpedo Boats Interchangeable

HMS	Completed	Builder
Dark Adventurer	1954	Saunders Roe (Anglesey) Ltd
Dark Agressor	1954	Saunders Roe (Anglesey) Ltd
Dark Antagonist	1955	Saunders Roe (Anglesey) Ltd
Dark Avenger	1955	Saunders Roe (Anglesey) Ltd
Dark Biter	1955	Saunders Roe (Anglesey) Ltd
Dark Buccaneer (ex-Dark Chaser)	1954	Vosper Ltd
Dark Clipper (ex-Dark Chieftain)	1955	Vosper Ltd
Dark Fighter	1955	J. Taylor
Dark Gladiator	1956	J. Taylor
Dark Hero	1957	McGrue Boats Ltd
Dark Highwayman (ex-Dark Crusader)	1955	Vosper Ltd
Dark Hunter	1954	J. Miller
Dark Hussar (ex-Dark Explorer)	1957	J.I. Thornycroft & Co.
Dark Intruder	1955	Morgan Giles Ltd
Dark Invader	1955	Morgan Giles Ltd
Dark Killer (ex-Dark Defender)	1956	J.I. Thornycroft & Co.
Dark Rover	1954	Vosper Ltd
Dark Scout	1958	Saunders Roe (Anglesey) Ltd

Dark Avenger. (Wright & Logan)

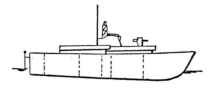

Right: 'Dark' Class 1956.

Below: Dark Rover. ((Vosper
Thornycroft)

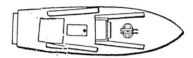

Specification

Displacement tons	64
Dimensions	71½ x 19¾ x 3¼ mean
Armament (as MGB)	One 4.5in, 25cal, one 40mm Bofors or two 40mm Bofors
Armament (as MTB)	One 40mm Bofors, four 21in torpedo tubes
Anti-submarine	One or two depth charge racks were fitted on some boats
Mines	HMS *Dark Antagonist* and possibly others of this class were used for minelaying with a capacity of six ground mines
Machinery	Twin diesel engines, 5,000shp
Speed	47 knots
Sea speed	40 knots
Fuel	8 tons oil
Complement	15

Note: Built of composite aluminium and wood. HMS *Dark Scout*, however, was built entirely of aluminium.

Cancellations: The following boats of the 'Dark' class were under construction to a greater or lesser extent when cancelled: *Dark Attacker*, *Dark Battler* and *Dark Bowman*. They were built by Saunders Roe (Anglesey) Ltd. *Dark Chaser*, *Dark Chieftain* and *Dark Crusader* were built by Vosper Ltd, *Dark Defender* and *Dark Explorer* by J.I. Thornycroft & Co. and *Dark Horseman* by McGrue Boats Ltd.

'Brave' Class Fast Patrol Boats

HMS	Completed	Builder
Brave Borderer	1960	Vosper Ltd
Brave Swordsman	1960	Vosper Ltd

Specification

Displacement tons	89, Full load 114
Dimensions	90pp 96wl 98¾ x 25½ x 6¼ mean
Armament (as MGB)	Two 40mm Bofors and two 21in side launched torpedoes
Armament (as MTB)	One 40mm Bofors and four 21in side launched torpedoes
Machinery	Three gas turbine propulsion units, 10,500shp
Speed	50 knots plus (trials)
Fuel	25 tons oil
Complement	20 or 22 as Senior Officers Ship

Note: Built with an aluminium hull and sheathed with glass fibre below the water line.

Gunnery note: The designed armament was one 3.3in turret-mounted gun with built-in stabilisation. Also one 40mm Bofors and two 21in torpedo tubes.

Designed for high speed minelaying.

Brave Swordsman. (Vosper Thornycroft)

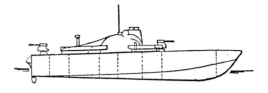

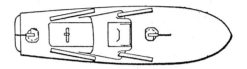

Right: 'Brave' Class 1959.

Below: Brave Swordsman.
(Vosper Thornycroft)

Chapter 18

Fast Training Boats

'Scimitar' Class Fast Training Boats

HMS	Completed	Builder
Cutlass	1970	Vosper Thornycroft
Sabre	1971	Vosper Thornycroft
Scimitar	1970	Vosper Thornycroft

Specification

Displacement tons	102
Dimensions	100 x 26½ x 6¼
Armament	Nil
Machinery	Two gas turbines and two diesel engines, for cruising in CODAG arrangement
	Gas turbines 9,000hp, diesel engines 750hp
Speed	40 knots
Range	425nm at 35 knots and 1500nm at 11½ knots
Complement	12

Note: Built of laminated wood and the design was developed from the 'Brave' Class FPBs. There is a facility for the fitting of a third gas turbine which would make these craft three-shafted. Built as training aids for comparison with the Soviet 'Osa' and 'Komar' Classes of Fast Attack Missile Craft.

HMS *Tenacity* Fast Patrol Craft

HMS	Completed	Commissioned	Builder
Tenacity	1972	1973	Vosper Thornycroft

Specification

Displacement tons	195, Full load 220
Dimensions	144½ x 26½ x 7¾
Armament	Two GPMG and small arms
Machinery	One Rolls-Royce Proteus Gas Turbine to each of three shafts, port, centre and starboard, all giving 12,750shp
Speed	40 knots

Also one Paxman Ventura diesel engine to port and starboard
shafts (only for cruising)

Speed	16 knots
Range	2,500nm at 15 knots
Complement	32

Design Note: HMS *Tenacity* was built as a 'one off' speculative venture as a design for a possible class of Fast Attack Missile Craft. Nothing came of that idea. However, after builders' trials and completion, she was purchased by the Ministry of Defence (for comparison with the Fast Training Boats of the 'Scimitar' Class. Since 1976, for various periods, she has been employed as a Fishery Protection and North Sea Patrol Craft.

Tenacity. (Vosper Thornycroft)

Opposite top: Cutlass, Sabre and *Scimitar*. (Vosper Thornycroft)

Opposite middle: Cutlass. (M. Lennon)

Opposite bottom: Sabre. (MOD)

Chapter 19

Hovercraft

BHN N7 Hovercraft

The BHN N7 Hovercraft type was built by the British Hovercraft Corporation. One of these was delivered to the Inter Service Hovercraft Trials Unit in April 1970 and given the number XW255.

Specification

Displacement tons	50 maximum weight, 33 light
Dimensions	78¼ x 45½ x 34 with a 5½ft skirt
Machinery	One gas turbine, 4,250shp which powers the propeller and provides the lift
Speed	60 knots
Complement	14 plus trials crew

Note: It is regrettable that all hovercraft, with the exception of the BH7 Mark 20 (for minesweeping) were phased out of service from December 1984.

BH7 Mk20 Hovercraft

The BH7 Mk20 Hovercraft was a development of the Mk2A but capable of minehunting/ minesweeping *inter alia*. To quote from BHC material: 'the minehunter craft with retractable sonars can detect underwater targets and dispose of them with the PAP104 remote control mine disposal vehicle or by the use of divers'.

In the minesweeping role the craft can tow the wire sweep, acoustic sweep, magnetic sweep or the combined magnetic and acoustic sweep.

Specification

All up weight	82 tons
Dimensions	94 x 45½ x 6½
Armament (Designed)	Two 30mm Rarden cannon DP
Machinery	One Allison 570k gas turbine geared to one CP air propeller, all giving 4,500shp
Fuel	7,000ipg JP3
Range Minehunting	100nm from base plus sixteen hours estimating 80nm
Range Minesweeping	100nm from base at towing speeds of 12/30 knots estimating 200nm
Complement	Over 4

BHN mk7. (British Hovercraft Corporation)

BH7 Mk20. (British Hovercraft Corporation)

BH7 Mk2A Hovercraft

BH7 Mark 2A Hovercraft were in service with the Royal Navy for two years from 1979 and were evaluated by the Hovercraft Trials Unit for a number of tasks, particularly minesweeping. The craft appeared to be most suited to this, having a low water pressure signature combined with the necessary high speed required for this task.
Builder: British Hovercraft Corporation Ltd.

Specification

All up weight	60 tons
Dimensions	76¾ x 45½ x 33 on landing pads
Machinery	One Rolls-Royce Marine Proteus gas turbine to one airscrew for propulsion and hover giving 4,250shp and 60 knots plus at maximum speed
Fuel	JP4/Kerosene, up to 11.8 tons can be carried
Endurance & Speed	Eight hours at 58 knots
Complement	14

SRN5 Hovercraft

Two of these hovercraft were deployed by the Royal Navy between 1965 to 1967 as Patrol Hovercraft during the Indonesian confrontation. They were operational in the Singapore Straits and patrolled turnabout, based on HMS *Terror* but were part of the Joint Services Hovercraft Unit (Far East).

Specification

Nominal gross tons	6½
Dimensions	38¾ x 23 x 13 (nominal height)
Armament	Two mg and similar weapons
Machinery	One gas turbine of 900shp powering the air propeller and lift fan
Speed (Designed)	66/62 knots
Range	205nm
Endurance	3½ hours at absolute maximum speed
Fuel	265ipg kerosene
Complement	12 but varied

Note: The SRN5 Hovercraft was the first air cushion vehicle in the world to go into quantity production.
Builder: British Hovercraft Corporation.

Note: Particulars of the above mentioned deployment may be found in the *Flight International* Air Cushion Vehicles Supplement of 23 February 1967.

BH7 Mk2A. (Source not known)

SRN5. (British Hovercraft Corporation)

 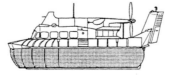 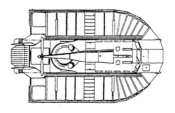

SRN5 Hovercraft.

SRN6 Hovercraft as Patrol Craft

HM Hovercraft	Completed	Builder
XV615–P236	1975	British Hovercraft Corporation
XV617–P237	1975	British Hovercraft Corporation
XV852–P235	1975	British Hovercraft Corporation

Specification

Operating Weight tons	10
Dimensions	48½ x 23 x 15
Machinery	One Rolls-Royce Gnome gas turbine to one propeller (this engine also supplies the lift under the rubber skirt) 900shp
Speed	50 knots or less
Range	200nm

Deployment note: These hovercraft were sent to Hong Kong in an attempt to curb the influx of immigrants and were on Anti-Immigration Patrol from 1979 until autumn 1982.

Weapon note: Small arms including GPMG and PN/SLR weapons.

Loss: HM Hovercraft P237 was damaged on rocks at Hong Kong on 19 January 1982 and became a constructive total loss while in hot pursuit of a speedboat.

SRN6. (British Hovercraft Corporation)

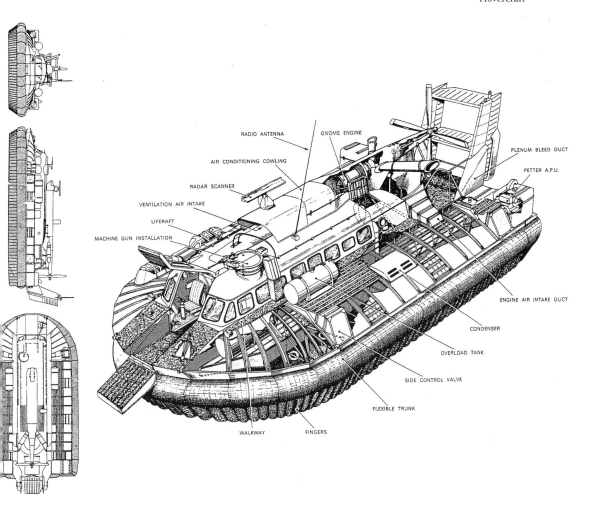

RADIO ANTENNA

GNOME ENGINE

PLENUM BLEED DUCT

AIR CONDITIONING COWLING

PETTER A.P.U.

RADAR SCANNER

VENTILATION AIR INTAKE

LIFERAFT

MACHINE GUN INSTALLATION

ENGINE AIR INTAKE DUCT

CONDENSER

OVERLOAD TANK

SIDE CONTROL VALVE

FLEXIBLE TRUNK

WALKWAY

FINGERS

SRN6 Hovercraft.

VT2 Hovercraft

Builder: Vosper Thornycroft

A VT2 was chartered by the Ministry of Defence (Navy) in 1976 and purchased outright in 1979.

The Type (VT2), along with other makes of hovercraft, was also tested as a troop carrier, A/S vessel, and assault craft. The most efficient use turned out to be minesweeping, due to the shallow draft of the VT2 and its great immunity from underwater detonations. The sweep may be streamed from the fore or after part of the hovercraft, brief particulars of which are:

Specification

Operating tons	100
Dimensions	100¼ x 43½ x 3 (still)
Propulsion/Lift	Two Proteus Gas Turbines giving 4,500shp at 60 knots
Range	300nm at full speed
Fuel	JP4 – 23½ tons

VT2. (Vosper Thornycroft)

Chapter 20

Seaward Defence Vessels

'Ford' Class Seaward Defence Vessels

HMS	Commenced	Completed	Builder
Aberford	1951	1954	Yarrow SB
Axford	1951	1955	Simons
Beckford	1951	1955	Simons
Brayford	1951	1954	Inglis
Bryansford	1951	1954	Inglis
Camberford	1952	1954	Vosper
Desford	1952	1954	Vosper
Droxford	1954	1954	Pimblott
Dubford	1951	1954	White
Gifford	1952	1954	Dunston
Glassford	1952	1955	Dunston
Greatford	1951	1954	White
Hinksford	1953	1956	Richards Ironworks
Ickford	1952	1955	Rowhedge Ironworks
Kingsford	1952	1955	Rowhedge Ironworks
Marlingford	1952	1955	Yarwood
Mayford	1953	1955	Richards Ironworks
Montford	1956	1958	Pimblott
Shalford	1951	195)4	Yarrow SB
Tilford	1956	1958	Vosper

Specification

Displacement tons	120, Full load 160
Dimensions	110, 117¼ x 20 x 5
Armament	One 40mm in a small bandstand forward of the wheelhouse
Anti-submarine	One Squid three-barrelled ahead-throwing mortar, and/or depth charge throwers and depth charge racks
Machinery	These vessels had triple shafts with Paxman engines to the outer shafts and a Foden engine to the middle shaft, all giving 1,100bhp at 18 knots with a sea speed of 15 knots
Complement	19
Fuel	23 tons oil fuel

Note: These small vessels were shorter in length than the 'D' Class Fairmiles of the Second World War but, nevertheless, they carried an armament sufficient to sink any submarine commissioned in the early 1950s. They were not, however, a great success, due to their small size. Their anti-submarine armament was equal to a 'Flower' Class Corvette and practically equal to a 'River' Class Frigate and, although designed for seaward defence of ports and harbours, in anything of a sea they would have been inadequate. These vessels were officially described as being able to detect, locate and destroy submarines. They were also fitted with the most modern and up-to-date electronic equipment available at that time.

Axford. (Wright & Logan)

Shalford. (Wright & Logan)

Chapter 21

Coastal Patrol Craft

'Bird' Class Patrol Craft

HMS	Commenced	Completed	Builder
Cygnet	1973	1976	Richard Dunston
Kingfisher	1973	1975	Richard Dunston
Peterel	1973	1977	Richard Dunston
Sandpiper	1973	1977	Richard Dunston

Specification

Displacement tons	194
Dimensions	120 x 21½ x 6½
Armament	One 40mm on the main deck, aft of all superstructure, two mg
Machinery	Two Paxman diesels giving 4,200bhp to two shafts
Speed	18 knots
Range	2,000nm at 14 knots
Oil Fuel	35 tons
Complement	19

Peterel. (Richard Dunston)

Kingfisher. (Richard Dunston)

Note: These vessels were an interim but expensive attempt at providing a dual purpose Fishery Protection and/or Platform Patrol Vessel. The design originated from Rescue Launches of the 'Seal' Class used by the Royal Air Force, but slightly enlarged.

'Attacker' Class Coastal Patrol Craft

HMS	Completed	Builder
Attacker	1983	Fairey Allday Marine
Chaser	1983	Fairey Allday Marine
Fencer	1983	Fairey Allday Marine
Hunter	1983	Fairey Allday Marine
Striker	1983	Fairey Allday Marine

Specification

Displacement tons	34
Dimensions	65½ x 17 x 4¾
Armament	Capacity for one 20mm single on the foredeck and a .5in mg on each bridge wing
Machinery	General Motors diesel engines, one to each of two shafts, all giving 1,300bhp
Speed	24 knots
Range	650nm at 20 knots
Fuel	1,200 imp gal
Fresh water	300 imp gal
Complement	11

Hunter. (Fairey Allday Marine)

Fencer. (Source not known)

Construction note: Built of GRP and GRP sandwich.

Intended use: For sea training by RNR Divisions and University RN Units. Normally of up to seven days duration.

Ex-Argentinian Coastal Patrol Craft HMS *Tiger Bay*

HMS	Ordered	Completed	Builder
Tiger Bay (ex-*Islas Malvinas*)	1978	1980	Blohm & Voss

Specification

Displacement tons	81
Dimensions	91¾ x 17¼ x 5½
Armament	Gun (as fitted), two 20mm AA
Machinery	MTU–92 diesel engines, one to each of two shafts giving, 2,100bhp
Speed	22 knots
Range	780nm at 18 knots and 1,200nm at 12 knots
Complement	15 (intended)

Note: One of a class of twenty built in West Germany for the Argentine Navy. Construction is of steel. Stabilisers are fitted. The *Islas Malvinas* was captured as a result of the South Atlantic campaign in 1982 to liberate the Falkland Islands from the Argentinian occupying forces. In January 1985 HMS *Tiger Bay* was laid up in HM Dockyard, Portsmouth.

Tiger Bay. (MOD)

HMS *Falkland Sound*

HMS	Completed	Builder
Falkland Sound (ex-*Yehuin*, ex-*Millerntor*)	1967	G.J. Hizler Schiff, Werft

Specification

Gross tons	495, Net reg. 149 tons
Dimensions	175½ x 37 x 11
Machinery	Two diesel engines one to each shaft, each giving 1,900bhp, fitted with controllable pitch propellers. 1 bow thrust unit
Speed	12 knots
Fuel	264 tons of oil fuel
RN Complement	12 plus

Note: *Yehuin* was captured by Crown Forces during the Falkland Islands campaign of 1982 and remedial repairs took place with the aid of HMS *Diligence*. After renaming to HMS *Falkland Sound* she was employed as a Patrol Vessel Tug and Salvage Vessel. She carried a variety of small arms for defence. Earlier in her career she had been employed in the North Sea as an oil rig support vessel, with the nickname of *Black Pig*.

'Guardian' Class Coastal Patrol Vessels, ex-North Sea Supply Vessels

HMS	Completed	Purchased	Builder
Guardian (ex-*Seaforth Champion*)	1974	1983	Cochrane
Protector (ex-*Seaforth Saga*)	1975	1983	Cochrane
Sentinel (ex-*Seaforth Warrior*)	1973	1983	Hasumer WG

Specification	*Guardian / Protector*	*Sentinel*
Displacement tons	1,992	1,688
Deadweight tons	1,030	1,191
Dimensions	191¼ x 38¾ x 14¾	202½ x 42½ x 17¾
Armament	Two 40mm Bofors 40/60 AA on single mountings	Two 40mm Bofors 40/60 AA on single mountings
Machinery	Two British Polar diesel engines to two shafts, giving 6,160bhp	Two diesel engines Type 12 MA53 AK to two shafts, giving 7,760bhp
Speed	13½ knots	13¾ knots
Cruising speed	11½ knots	11½ knots
Range	13,500nm at 11½ knots	8,800nm at 11½ knots
Complement	24	26

Note: These three vessels were built as North Sea oil rig supply ships and purchased for the Royal Navy in 1983. They were used as Coastal Patrol Vessels for the Falkland Islands.

Guardian. (MOD)

Sentinel. (MOD)

'Peacock' Class Coastal Patrol vessels (Hong Kong)

HMS	Commenced	Completed	Builder
Peacock	1982	1983	Hail Russell
Plover	1982	1981	Hall Russell
Starling	1982	1981	Hall Russell
Swallow	1983	1984	Hall Russell
Swift	1983	1985	Hall Russell

Specification

Displacement tons	710
Dimensions	206¼ x 32¼ x 18 deep
Armament	One 76mm Oto Melara DP, Automatic and small arms
Machinery	Crossley–Pielstick diesels, one to each of two shafts, giving 7,094bhp
Speed	25 knots
Range	2500nm at 15 knots
Complement	42
Aircraft	These vessels had a built-in refuelling capacity for helicopters, also a winching system

Swallow. (MOD)

Peacock. (MOD)

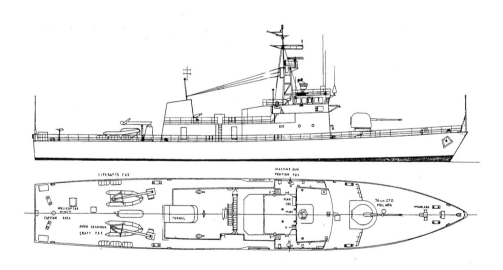

Coastal Patrol Vessels (Hong Kong) 'Peacock' Class.

Class note: The Secretary of State for Defence announced that this type of patrol vessel would be manned by the Royal Navy for service at Hong Kong and would replace the ageing 'Ton' Class Minesweepers, which were presently carrying out anti–infiltration, fishery protection and patrol duties at the Crown Colony.

'Archer' Class (P2000) Coastal Patrol Craft

HMS	Completed★	Builder
Archer	1986	All by Watercraft
Biter	1985	
Blazer	1988	
Charger	1988	
Dasher	1988	
Example+	1985	
Exploit+	1986	
Explorer+	1988	
Express+	1988	
Puncher	1988	
Pursuer	1988	
Ranger	1988	
Smiter	1986	
Trumpeter	1988	

Archer. (Watercraft Ltd)

Specification

Displacement tons	44
Dimensions	68¼ x 19 x 6
Armament	One 20mm AA (provision for) on the foredeck
Machinery	Two shaft diesel engines all giving 1,590/1,380bhp
Speed	22½ knots
Range	500nm at 15 knots
Complement	11

Note: All built for use by the Naval Reserves with the 'Ex' boats for the Royal Naval Auxiliary Service.

Messrs Watercraft became economically unviable, leaving the latter nine hulls to be fitted out by Vosper Thornycroft (UK) Ltd. All were heavier than anticipated by about 6 tons.

Chapter 22

Offshore Patrol Vessels

'Island' Class Offshore Patrol Vessels

HMS	Completed	Builder
Alderney	1979	All built by Hall Russell of Aberdeen
Anglesey	1979	
Guernsey	1977	
Jersey	1976	
Lindisfarne	1978	
Orkney	1977	
Shetland	1977	

Specification

Displacement tons	925 tons, Full load 1,260 tons
Dimensions	195½ x 34½ x 14
Armament (As built)	One 40/70 Bofors DP
	Two 7.62DP mg

Jersey. (Ton Class Association)

Shetland. (Ton Class Association)

Machinery	Two Ruston diesel engines, each giving 2,190bhp to a variable pitch propeller
Speed	16 knots but 14 knots on one shaft
Range	11,100nm
Complement	Up to 39

Design note: These vessels derived from the *Jura* and *Westra*, built at the same yard for the Scottish Home Department. *Jura* was leased to the MOD for a period and commissioned as an HM ship, being armed and deployed as the above on Fishery Protection and similar duties, all proving to be better sea boats than the 'Bird' Class of 1975.

Deep bilge keels were fitted to the first five of this class but *Lindisfarne* and *Orkney* received stabilisers in lieu.

'Castle' Class Offshore Patrol Vessels

HMS	Launched	Completed	Builder
Dumbarton Castle	1981	1982	Both built by Hall Russell at Aberdeen
Leeds Castle	1980	1981	

Specification

Displacement	1,450 tons
Dimensions	265 x 37 x 11¼
Armament (Designed)	One 76mm DP Oto Melara turreted piece

Dumbarton Castle. (Navpic)

Leeds Castle. (TCA)

Armament (Completion)	One 40/70 Bofors DP, 7.62mm DP mg, mounted according to deployment etc.
Machinery	Two Ruston diesel engines each giving 2,820bhp to a variable pitch propeller
Speed	20 knots
Range	12,000nm at 12 knots
Fuel	180 tons
Complement	50 plus

Note: Both of the above served actively in the Falklands War against Argentina and over the years one or both has been duty Guard Ship in the Islands. Fitted for RAS and with a helideck, also non-retractable active fin type stabilisers. This is a logical development from the 'Island' Class Offshore Patrol Vessels. Also adapted for minelaying, carrying eight on the after main deck (see note below).

Note: For further particulars of these vessels see page 63 of this author's *Mine Warfare Vessels of the Royal Navy —1908 to Date* (published by Airlife Ltd in 1993).

'River' Class Offshore Patrol Vessels

HMS	Commenced	Completed	Builder
Mersey	2002	2004	Vosper Thornycroft for all three of this class
Severn	2002	2003	
Tyne	2001	2003	

Specification

Displacement	1,700 tons
Dimensions	260¾ x 44½ x 12½
Armament	One 20mm DP and two 7.62mm mg
Machinery	Two Ruston diesel engines, both giving 2,800bhp, with controllable pitch propellers and a bow thrusters
Speed	20 knots plus
Range	5,000nm
Complement	43 plus

Note: Built and owned by the builders but leased to MOD with an option to purchase one or all after five years during which period they are maintained by Vosper Thornycroft. Intended to be at sea more than alongside the dockyard wall. Not fitted with a helideck but space aft on the main deck for helicopter winching of stores and personnel. Intended to fulfil the duties of the 'Island' Class with just three vessels (there were seven of that previous class).

Mersey. (Navpic)

Severn. (Navpic)

Chapter 23

Coastal Jetfoil

HMS *Speedy*

HMS	Commenced	Completed	Builder
Speedy	1978	1980+	Boeing (Seattle)

Shipped to the UK and fitted out by Vosper Thornycroft

Specification

Displacement tons	117		
Armament (designed)	Two 7.62 mg on single mountings		
Machinery	Two Allison 501 gas turbines powering the waterjets giving 7,560hp when foil-borne. Two Detroit GM diesel engines, one to each shaft when hull-borne, all giving 1,100bhp		
Dimensions	Hull-borne	Foils retracted	Foil-borne
	90 x 30 x 17	101 x 30 x 6	90 x 30 x 8
Speed	5 to 15 knots		40 knots
Range	3,500nm		560nm
Fuel	23 tons		
Complement	18		

Note: HMS *Speedy*, at 12/1982, was for disposal. She was the first and only hydrofoil of this type from an intended class of twelve. In September 1981 she was attached to the Fishery Protection and North Sea Patrol Squadron at Rosyth. In 1982 was used in minesweeping/minelaying trials when based at Portsmouth, but apparently did not prove satisfactory.

Speedy. (Vosper Thornycroft)

Chapter 24

Ex-RAF Marine Craft

HMS *Redpole* Ex–Royal Air Force Marine Branch Craft

HMS	Completed	Acquired	Builder
Redpole	1970	1985	Fairmile Const. (Berwick-upon-Tweed)

Specification (as built)

Displacement	159
Dimensions	120 x 23 x 6½
Armament	Nil
Machinery	Two diesel engines, one to each shaft all giving 4,000bhp
Speed	21 knots
Range	2,200nm at 12 knots
Fuel	31 tons diesel fuel
Complement	17

Note: With the discontinuation of the Marine Branch and its craft of the Royal Air Force a number of the various craft as described above and below have been acquired by the Royal Navy and adapted for RN use and renamed. Originally built as long range recovery and support craft.

Redpole. (MOD)

HMS	Completed	Acquired	Builder
Cormorant (ex-*Sunderland*)	1976	1985	James & Stone (Brightlingsea)
Hart (ex-*Stirling*)	1976	1985	James & Stone (Brightlingsea)

Specification (as built)

Displacement	48, Full load 60
Dimensions	77¾ x 18 x 5
Armament	Nil
Machinery	Two diesel engines, one to each shaft, all giving 2,000bhp
Speed:	22 knots
Range	500nm at 21 knots
Fuel	10 tons diesel fuel
Complement	9

Note: See notes above. Originally built as Rescue and Target Towing Launches.

Hart and *Cormorant*. (MOD)

Chapter 25

M160 Class Patrol Boats

In 2002, information was released by MOD via the *Navy News* that, in 1987/1988, two new construction Patrol Boats had been placed and were operational on Lough Neagh in Ulster. The Lough is the largest area of fresh water in Northern Ireland, with no navigable access to the sea.

The two craft were manned by the Royal Navy and Royal Marines and based at Masserene Barracks, Antrim, in a secure basin under control of the military.

The builder of these craft is Halmatic Ltd of Portsmouth and brief particulars follow below:

Specification

Dimensions	52½ x 15½ x 4¾
Machinery	Particulars not given. However, from the photograph, it may be assumed that twin engines, one to each shaft, are fitted of petrol/diesel type.
Speed	25 knots plus
Complement	4, plus space for additional 30 persons for a short time/distance

Note: Used for counter-terrorism operations in the province. Armament may be assumed to be sidearms rpgs and mgs etc. The names recall the Steam Gun Boats of the Second World War, being called HMS *Grey Fox* and HMS *Grey Wolf*.

It is believed that both craft have differences in appearance and it is not known which craft is shown on the photograph.

Re-naming note: In January 2003 *Grey Fox* became *Scimitar* and *Grey Wolf* became *Sabre*. Both were deployed at Gibraltar.

M160
Patrol Boat.
(MOD)

Chapter 26

Royal Marine Craft 1994 *et seq.*

Fast Interceptor Craft (RM)

HMS	Completed	Builder
FIC1	1994	Halmatic
FIC2	1994	Halmatic

Specification

Full load	12½ tons
Dimensions	47¾ x 9¼ x 4¼
Armament	LMG/MMG and small arms
Machinery	Seatek diesels to twin shafts, all giving 1,160bhp
Speed	45 knots
Range	225nm at 45 knots
Complement	2 plus

Notes: Designated a FIC145 Class.
The construction is of Kevlar and GRP for the entire craft.
Normally manned and used by members of the Royal Marines.

FIC145. (Halmatic)

Fast Interceptor Craft (RM)(VSV)

A small number of these craft were completed by Halmatic Ltd far the Royal Marines in 2002.

Specification

Known as the VSV – 16m 145 Class

Displacement	7¼ tons
Dimensions	52½ x 91¼ x 31¼
Armament	According to requirements, such as GPMGs and 20mm etc
Machinery	Twin 660/750bhp diesel
Fuel	3000 litres
Speed	60 knots plus
Complement	Up to 3 with passenger space

A follow up version, also by Halmatic Ltd, has a brief specification:

Known as the VSV – 22m

Displacement	19¾ tons
Dimensions	75 x 14¼ x 3¾
Armament	According to requirements, such as GPMGs, RPGs, and 20mm
Machinery	Twin 1,000/2,000bhp diesel
Fuel	In excess of the 145 Class
Speed	60 knots plus
Complement	Up to 3 with passenger space

Note: Similar in size to the Coastal Motor Boats of the First World War but with enhanced performance.

Both types are air portable and designed for covert and patrol tasks.

VSV Craft. (Halmatic)

FIC VSV Craft. (Halmatic)

Royal Marines Hovercraft.
(Griffon Hovercraft, A,
Hotham, MOD)

Assault Hovercraft (RM)

HM	Completed	Builder
C21	1993	Griffon Ltd
C22	1993	Griffon Ltd
C23	1994	Griffon Ltd
C24	1994	Griffon Ltd

Specification

Full load	6¾ tons
Dimensions	36 x 15 x 1½ to beaching level
Armament	One 7.62mm mg
Machinery	Deutz diesel giving 355bhp
Speed	40 knots
Range	300nm at 25 knots
Fuel	284 litres
Complement	2 plus a load of 2 tons or 16 troops embarked with full equipment

Note: Constructed of aluminium and normally transported by an amphibious warfare
vessel or aircraft. Should be able to operate at top speed on water up to sea state 4.
Operating permissible over ice and mud shingle dunes and grass, but this would limit
the speed. Over tarmac or concrete a high speed would be attainable.

Designated Type 2000TDX(M)(LCPA).

Have already been used by the Royal Marines overseas for trials and operations.

Appendix 1

Enemy Losses Attributable to HM Coastal Forces

Ship/Type	Flag	Date and Place	HM Ship(s)
First World War			
Petro Pavlovsk (Battleship)	Russian (Bolshevik)	18 August 1919 Kronstadt Naval Base	Coastal Motor Boats
Saria Svobodi (Battleship)	"	"	"
Bogatyr (Cruiser)	"	"	"
Pamiat Azova (Submarine Depot Ship)	"	"	"
Konigsberg (Cruiser)	German	11 July 1915 Rufuji River	HMS *Mersey* and *Severn*
Hermann von Wissman (Lake Gun Boat)	"	30 May 1915 Lake Nyasa	HMS *Guedolen*
Hedwig von Wissman (Lake Gun Boat)	"	9 February 1916 Lake Tanganyika	HMS *Fifi* and HM Launch *Mimi*
Kingani (Lake Gun Boat)	"	26 December 1915 Lake Tanganyika	HM Launches *Mimi* and *Tou tou*
G 88 (Destroyer)	"	7/8 April 1917 off Zeebrugge	Coastal Motor Boat
Second World War			
Iltis (Torpedo Boat)	"	13/14 May 1942 off Boulogne	HM MTBs
Seeadlar (Torpedo Boat)	"	13/14 May 1942 off Boulogne	HM MTBs
T27 (Torpedo Boat)	"	29 April 1944 off Boulogne	HM MTBs & HMCS *Haida* (Destroyer)
Komet (Armed Merchant Cruiser)	"	14 October 1942 off Cherbourg	HM MTB236
Santorre Santarosa (Submarine)	Italian	20 January 1943 off Tripoli	HM MTB260
Flutto (Submarine)	"	11 July 1943 Straits of Messina	HM MTBs 640, 651 and 670
U561 (Submarine)	German	12 July 1943 Straits of Messina	HM MTB81
Niobe (Cruiser ex-Yugoslav)	"	21/22 December 1943 Adriatic Sea	HM MTBs
TA25 (Torpedo Boat) (ex-Italian *Intrepido*)	"	14/15 June 1944 west of Spezia	HM MTBs
TA30 (Torpedo Boat) (ex-Italian *Dragone*)	"	14/15 June 1944 west of Spezia	HM MTBs
TA45 (Torpedo Boat) (ex-Italian *Spika*)	"	13 April 1945 Gulf of Fiume	HM MTBs

Many other vessels were sunk or damaged by Coastal Forces but particulars are not available.

Appendix 2

Coastal Forces Losses

Cause	HM Ships	Total
Aircraft Attack	*Cicala, Dragonfly, Grasshopper, Ladybird* and *Mosquito* CH9, CMBs 40, 42, 47, LCF(3)13, HDML1011, MGBs 19, 98, 648, MLs 160, 252, 353, 579, 835, MTBs 33, 37, 39, 40, 67, 73, 77, 108, 213, 214, 216, 217, 288, 308, 310, 312	35
Attacked in error by allied aircraft	MTBs 448, 708, 734.	3
Attacked in error by allied naval vessel	MTB 732	1
Capsized	TB90	1
Captured by the enemy	*Peningat* MGB78, ML306, MTBs 314, 631	5
Collision	*Hazard*, CMBs 11, 18A, 71A, LCS(L)(1)201, MA/SB30, MLs 121, 183, 230, 251, 356, MGB62, MTBs 29, 63, 64, 68, 93, 230, 248, 352, 412, 430, 690, 707, P12	25
Constructive total loss	*Blackfly, Gnat, Puffin*, HDML1019, Hovercraft XV617, MA/SB3, MLs 97, 127, 147, 229, 285, 460, MGBs 99, 109, MTB493	15
Contacted floating torped	ML403	1
Destroyed when incomplete by aircraft attack	HDMLs 1092, 1093, 1094, 1095	4
Expended as a target	CMB90BD, MTBs 243, 635	3
Fire	CMBs 2, 10, 39B, 99ED, 114D, HDML1147, MLs 19, 40, 52, 55, 64, 133, 149, 169, 196, 242, 265, 278, 287, 431, 434, 521, 534. MGBs 90, 92, MTBs 28, 255, 301, 338, 345, 387, 438, 444, 459, 461, 462, 465, 601, 626, 686, 776, 789, 791, 798	44
Grounded/Wrecked	HDMLs 1015, 1054, 1119, 1388, LCS(M)(3)69, MLs 152, 197, 219, 247, 421, 591, 631, 905, MGB2007, MTBs 61, 287, 371, TB4	20

Heavy weather	*Tou Tou*, HDMLs 1083, 1100, 1121, 1179, 1380, LCG(L)(3) s 15, 16, MLs 18, 62, 191, 288, 566, MGB64, MTBs 6, 242,267	18
Internal explosion	*Glatton*, HDML1060, MGB501, MTB 715	4
Lost as deck cargo	HDMLs 1003, 1037, 1090, 1153, 1157, 1212, 1244, MLs 230, 253, 255, 540, 541, MTBs 284, 285	14
Mined	*Cricket, Erebus, Jason, Pintail, Speedy*, HDMLs 1057, 1069, 1154, 1226, 1417, LCF(3)18, LCS(R)457 M21, MLs 103, 108,109, 111, 127, 144, 210, 216, 258, 313, 443, 466, 561, 563, 870, 890, 916, MGBs 12, 17, 2007, MTBs 15, 16, 17, 30, 41, 87, 106, 218, 222, 264, 311, 463, 640, 644, 655, 657, 663, 672, 697, 705, 710, 782, P26, TBs 10, 11, 12	59
Not known	CMB820, HDMLs 1030, 1039, 1289, LCS(M)(1)1, LCS(M)(3)s 42, 47, 48, 54, 59, ML98, MTBs 80, 203, 215, 261, 262, 605, 625, 712	19
Scuttled/Own forces	*Moth, Robin, Tern*, CMBs 8, 50, HDMLs 1096, 1102, 1103, 1104, 1167, 1169, 1170, Ms 25, 27, MLs 254, 362, 363, 364, 365, 372, 373, 374, 375, 376, 377, 432, 433, 436, 437, MTBs 7, 8, 9, 10, 11, 27, 105	36
Shore batteries	CMBs 24A, 62BD, 79A, HDML1259, M30, MLs 110, 156, 177, 192, 262, 267, 268, 270, 306, 314, 424, 446, 447, 457, 562, MGB641, MTBs 74, 636, 665,	24
Surface action	*Peterel, Raglan, Scorpion*, CMBs 1, 33A, HDMLs 1062, 1063, 1227, LCS(M)(1)17, 23, M28, MLs 129, 130, 310, 311, 328, 335, 358, 474, MGBs 18, 76, 79, 110, 5001, MTBs 12, 43, 44, 47, 220, 227, 241, 316, 347, 356, 357, 360, 372, 417, 434, 606, 622, 639, 666, 669, 671, 681, SGB7	47
Structural failure	MTB101	1
Torpedoed	*Niger*, HDML1163, M15, ML339	4

Landing Craft Support other than those mentioned in the above loss categories

Lost at Anzio	LCF(M)(3).6	1
Lost off Burma	LCS(M)(2)30, LCS(M)(3)148	2
Lost in India	LCS(M)(1)16	1
Lost off Normandy	LCS(M)(3)s 75, 101, 101, 103, 108, 114, LCF(2)1, LCF(4)31, LCG(L)(4)s 764, 831, 1062	16
Lost at North Africa	LCS(M)(1)s 11, 14, LCS(M)(2)28	3
Lost at Tobruk	LCS(M)(1)s 4, 6, 15, 18, 19, 22	6
Lost off Walcheren	LCS(L)(2)s 252, 256, 258, LGF(4)s 37, 38, LCG(L)(3)s 1, 2, LCG(M)(1)s 101, 102	9
Lost off Dieppe	LCS(M)9, LCF(2)2	2

Appendix 3

Thames Sea Forts Royal Navy Manned – Second World War

HM Fort	Commenced	Completed	Builder
Knock John	1941	1942	Sir Alex Gibb & Partners
Roughs Tower	1941	1942	Red Lion Wharf, North Fleet
Sunk Head	1941	1942	With fitting out at Tilbury
Tongue Sand	1941	1942	"

Specification

Displacement tons	4,500
Protection	Plastic and steel armour
Armament	Two 3.7in Army HA guns
	Two 40mm Bofors DP, PAC rockets, 20mm DP HA number per fort varies, .303" MG number per fort varies
Machinery	Diesel generators and similar, plus searchlights
Equipped	Two whalers, radar, W/T, ammunition various calibres
	The crew messing, sleeping, control rooms, stores were in one vertical tower
	The PO messing, officer sleeping, PO sleeping, magazines were in one vertical tower plus engine room and fuel all on different levels. The CO's cabin was in the superstructure. The superstructure crossing the two towers was of steel and supported all guns inc. radar and W/T plus compartments for officers' mess, galley and galley store. Each tower had seven decks
Construction	Built on-shore and fitted out there with a concrete base all reinforced the attachment of the towers and the steel superstructure. Floated out and beached in adequate depth of water for stability with at least thirty-five of the towers above HWMOST
Comment	The perfect example of a stationary HM ship in coastal waters under naval command and guarding the seaway to and from London Sheerness and Chatham
Complement	120 officers and men (Royal Navy and Royal Marines)
Nomenclature	Originally known as Thames Estuary Special Defence Units

HM Fort *Knock John*.
(Imperial War Museum)

Bibliography

The War at Sea Captain S.W. Roskill DSC RN HMSO

Japanese Warships of World War I A.J. Watts, Ian Allan Ltd

Janes Fighting Ships – various editions, F.T. Jane Sampson, Low & Marston

Warships of World War II H.T. Lenton & J.J. Colledge, Ian Allan Ltd

Transactions of the Royal Institution of Naval Architects, Various Years, RINA London

Janes Pocket Book 9 Denis Archer, MacDonald & Janes

British Warships 1914–1919 F.J. Dittmar & J.J. Colledge, Ian Allan Ltd

Royal Naval Coastal Forces A.J.D North, Almark Publications

German Warships of World War II J.C. Taylor, Ian Allan Ltd

Warships of the Royal Navy Captain J.E. Moore RN, MacDonald & Janes

British Escort Ships H.T. Lenton, MacDonald & Janes

A Dictionary of Ships of the Royal Navy of the Second World War John Young, Patrick Ltd

Ships of the Royal Navy J.J. Colledge, David & Charles

Allied Escort Ships of World War II Peter Elliott, MacDonald & Janes

Fast Attack Craft Phelan Brice, MacDonald & Janes

Conways All the Worlds Fighting Ships 1860–1905 Edited by A. Gardiner Conway, Maritime Press

Warships of World War I H.M. le Fleming, Ian Allan Ltd

Axis Submarines A.J. Watts, MacDonald & Janes

Allied Submarines A.J. Watts, MacDonald & Janes

Destroyers of the Royal Navy 1893–1981 Maurice Cocker, Ian Allan Ltd

Observers Directory of Royal Naval Submarines 1901–1982 M.P. Cocker, Frederick Warne (Publishers) Ltd

Frigates, Sloops & Patrol Vessels of the Royal Navy 1900 to date M.P. Cocker, Westmoreland Gazette

100 Years of Specialized Shipbuilding & Engineering K.C. Barnaby, Hutchinson

Yarrow 1865–1977 A. Borthwick & Others, Yarrow (Shipbuilders) Ltd

Mine Warfare Vessels of the Royal Navy M.P. Cocker, Airlife Ltd

Index